PERL IN YOUR HANDS

For Beginner's In PERL Programming

Gokul Amuthan S

ISBN-13 : 9781530959631
ISBN-10 : 1530959632

Available in amazon.com and other domains also.
Published by Gokul Amuthan S.

PREFACE

Writing a book is an art, and I am pleased to bring forward one of my art to your perspective. I have comprised my entire knowledge of PERL into this book. And I hope it would be a trustful guide in the world of PERL scripting.

I would like to extend my sincere thanks to the persons who have helped and motivated me in completing this book. And all the best to the readers who are beginners in PERL.

GOKULAMUTHAN S

This page is intentionally left blank

INTRODUCTION

The aim of this book is to provide a self-tutorial for the programmers out in the world who is in need of learning this language for the better development of their career.

I have covered most of the basic concept in PERL and appended scripts with their outcomes, so no problem on your part to judge the output. How to use this book? The Perl script is written after the title "Script" and the execution output is provided along with the Script under the title "Output".

This book is more than enough for novices and to show off in PERL. And I always welcome comments and suggestions on my work. The best way to contact me is via email. You can mail me through ***gokul.amuthan.s@gmail.com****. Wishing you good luck to proceed in your career.*

This page is intentionally left blank

TABLE OF CONTENTS

BACKGROUND OF PERL

PERL or **P**ractical **E**xtraction and **R**eporting **L**anguage is a high level language written originally by Larry Wall. The Perl semantics is largely based on C language, but it also inherits most of the interesting features of SED, AWK, UNIX shell and variety of other tools. Perl gained its popularity through its amazing capability of processing the text. This makes it useful in system administration, database access, networking, internet programming and so on.

The original popularity of the Perl is when CGI scripting and regular expressions were included.

The basic principle of Perl is based on the TIMTOWTDI (pronounced as 'Tim Toady') – There Is More Than One Way To Do It- syndrome, which is contrast of Python which is based on "There should be one-- and preferably only one --obvious way to do it". The current stable release in market is 5.21 which is included with some specific features.

Version of Perl:

1. **Perl 0** (1987) introduced by Larry Wall for his associates
2. **Perl 1** (Jan, 1988) introduced in the programming world
3. **Perl 2** (Jun, 1988) introduced by Harry Spencer by adding regular expression package

4. **Perl 3** (1989) introduced with ability to handle binary data

5. **Perl 4** (1991) added with first Camel book written by Larry Wall, Tom Christiansen and Randal L Schwartz

6. **Perl 4.036** (1993) is the last stable version of Perl 4

7. **Perl 5** (1994) is a complete rewrite with numerous features

Perl source code is open and free, hence anybody can download the C code which creates an interpreter. Some of commonly used Perl interpreter are Active State Perl and Strawberry Perl. If you have Cygwin installed, it also has a default Perl interpreter in it, where you can execute your code.

In this book I preferred to Active State Perl version 5.20.2, which you can download freely from **www.activestate.com/activeperl**. Once the setup is downloaded and installed you are ready to go. Make sure you have the path variable enabled with Perl interpreter.

VERIFYING THE INSTALLATION

Once you have installed your Perl interpreter, open your command prompt and type in the command **perl –version** or **perl –v** and if you get text as below then yippee you have your installation successful,

```
G:\Programs\Perl>perl -version

This is perl 5, version 20, subversion 2 (v5.20.2) built for MSWin32-x86-mult:
hread-64int
(with 1 registered patch, see perl -V for more detail)

Copyright 1987-2015, Larry Wall

Binary build 2001 [298913] provided by ActiveState http://www.ActiveState.com
Built Mar 19 2015 15:26:52

Perl may be copied only under the terms of either the Artistic License or the
GNU General Public License, which may be found in the Perl 5 source kit.

Complete documentation for Perl, including FAQ lists, should be found on
this system using "man perl" or "perldoc perl".  If you have access to the
Internet, point your browser at http://www.perl.org/, the Perl Home Page.

G:\Programs\Perl>
```

SAVING AND EXECUTING SCRIPTS

All the Perl scripts are saved with extension ".pl". To execute your script you simply need to type the following command, **perl filename.pl**.

```
G:\Programs\Perl>perl p1.pl
Numbers         2       3

G:\Programs\Perl>
```

Another alternative on Windows platform, is that you can convert the script to a batch file using **pl2bat** and execute.

```
G:\Programs\Perl>pl2bat p1.pl

G:\Programs\Perl>p1
Numbers         2       3
```

p1.bat

```
@rem = '--*-Perl-*--

@echo off

if "%OS%" == "Windows_NT" goto WinNT

perl -x -S "%0" %1 %2 %3 %4 %5 %6 %7 %8 %9

goto endofperl

:WinNT

perl -x -S %0 %*

if NOT "%COMSPEC%" ==
"%SystemRoot%\system32\cmd.exe" goto endofperl

if %errorlevel% == 9009 echo You do not have
Perl in your PATH.

if errorlevel 1 goto
script_failed_so_exit_with_non_zero_val 2>nul

goto endofperl

@rem ';

#!perl

#line 15

use 5.18.2;

use strict;

use warnings;


sub prints

{

      print "Numbers\t";
```

```
}
prints;
print "\t2","\t3\n";
__END__
:endofperl
```

The .bat is auto created on executing the command **pl2bat p1.pl**. This is quite easy to run through command line as if it's a command and we can ignore annoying conventional way with extension.

This page is intentionally left blank

BUILDING BLOCKS OF PERL

Variables: A variable is just a storage area, which contains valuable information's. Perl variables do not have any datatypes. It can have any value associated with it. Perl supports three categories of variables namely,

Scalar, which is the basic type that can hold either integer or strings or real values. A scalar variable is declared as **$var_name=value;**, where value can be a number or a string.

Arrays, which is simply a collection of scalar variables (need not be of homogeneous scalar's i.e., same type of valued scalars). An array is declared as **@arr_name = (val_1, ... val_n);**, where val_1, ... val_n can be either numbers or strings.

Hashes, which is a list of pair of key and respective values. Using the key the value can be gained. A hash is declared as **%hash_name = (key_1 => val_1, ... key_n => val_n);**, where key_1, ... key_n and val_1, ... val_n are scalars.

The scope of the variable can be controlled by three other keywords, **our,** which treats the variable as globally available; **my,** which treats the variable is available only in that particular scope; **local,** does not create local variable rather dynamically changes the value of the variable. I personally recommend not to use local modifier to your variable as it can be messier and unsafe.

Operators: An operator does operation on the values or variables. All the operators in C are allowed except few are ignored. The list of operator will be discussed in later part of the section

Statements: A statement is a single line in our script which enables us to control the execution flow.

Subroutines (Functions): A group of code collected under a single name which can be called multiple number of times. Subroutines are useful when some set of codes are repeatedly executed in script.

Modules: A collection of useful subroutines grouped under a single name which allows us to reuse them whenever they are required. They are written in "**.pm**" file.

Note that some modules that are already written for convenience of programmers can be downloaded from CPAN which is freely available. This can be done using **Perl Package Manager (PPM)**. The **ppm** command opens the Perl Package Manager as shown below

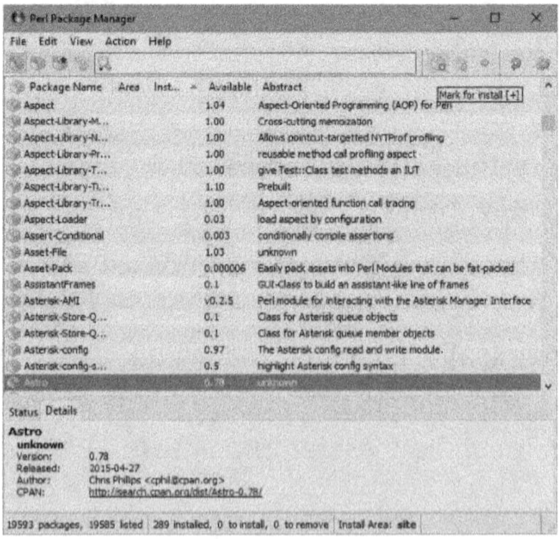

OPERATORS LIST

1) Arrow (Dereference) operator (->)

2) Auto increment and decrement operator (++ --)

3) Exponential operator (**)

4) Unary logical operator (~ | ^ &)

5) Regular Expression binding (=~)

6) Binary Arithmetic operator (+ - * / %)

7) X-Repetition operator (x)

8) String concatenation operator (.)

9) Shift operator (>> <<)

10) Relational operator (< > <= >=)

11) Relational operator (lt gt le ge)

12) Equality operator (== !=)

13) Equality operator (eq ne)

14) Comparison operator (<=> cmp)

15) Binary logical operator (&& || !)

16) Binary logical operator (and or not xor)

17) Range operators (.. ...)

18) Ternary (Conditional) operator (?:)

19) Compound assignment operator (+= -= /= &= ...etc.)

20) List (Array, Hash) operators (=> ,)

Note that the precedence is same as in other languages, except for the list operation which is discussed below.

Precedence of Terms and List

The terms are evaluated from left to right. The terms include variables, quotes, expressions, subroutine calls. List such as parameter list are evaluated in according to precedence of terms

Script

```
use 5.18.2;

use strict;

use warnings;

sub str

{

        print "Result is ";

}

my $a=3,$b=4;

print(($a+$b)."\n",str);
```

Output

```
G:\Programs>perl sample.pl

Result is 7

1
```

In the previous script, we can see that the parameters of the print function are evaluated from right to left. Seeing code we thought the result would be "7" and on next line string will be printed but it is not what happened. Now you would have a curious question raised on your mind that why that "1" is printed? It is due to successful execution of subroutine "str". And from this we should learn that without knowing the precedence of the terms, we will have a gobbled up output.

Script

```
use 5.18.2;

strict;

use warnings;

$a=2;

print "$a^$a\t",$a**++$a;

#Perl executes parameter from right to left
```

Output

```
G:\ Programs\Perl>perl p2.pl

2^2     27
```

In the above script see how the output is gobbled up, yielding 2 power 2 is 27, but what we expected was 3 power 3 as 27. So care must be taken while writing these type of statements

Some of functions that act as named unary operators are alarm, chdir, chr, chroot, cos, defined, do, delete, eval, exit, gethostbyname, getnetbyname, goto, hex, lc, localtime, lock, lstat, my, oct, our, rand, require, return, rmdir, scalar, sin, sleep, sqrt, srand, stat, uc, undef. If the above is used along with a parenthesis then automatically its precedence raises.

Script

```
use 5.18.2;

strict;

use warnings;

$a=2;

print  "$a^$a=",$a**$a,"\nValue  of  a  now  is
",++$a;
```

Output

```
G:\ Programs\Perl>perl p2a.pl

2^2=4

Value of a now is 3
```

See here the output remained intact and not ambiguous. So it's better for a beginner to avoid clubbed up statements. This may cost you by increasing your line of code but, hey a good working lengthy code is better than nonsensical code.

SUBROUTINES

The subroutines can be defined by the user by following the below syntax:-

sub subroutine_name

{

#statements;

}

A Perl script can have many user defined subroutines as per their wish. The following is an example of user defined subroutines.

Script

```
use 5.10.1;

strict;

use warnings;

sub prints

{

	print "Numbers\t";

}

prints;

print "\t2","\t3\n";
```

Output

```
G:\ Programs\Perl>perl p1.pl
Numbers		2	3
```

It's not necessary to indent statement inside the subroutines, it just a formatting style that I would prefer for easy identification of unbalanced parenthesis.

Script

```
sub one
{
	print "\nFirst one";
	return 1;
}
sub two
{
	print "\nSecond";
	my $a=4;
	$a+=2;
}
my $a=one; # can be called as one() also
my $b=two;
print "\nFirst sub routine returns $a";
print "\nSecond sub routine returns $b";
```

Output

```
G:\ Programs>perl sample2.pl

First one

Second

First sub routine returns 1

Second sub routine returns 6
```

A subroutine can return value by either explicitly mention return keyword or the last computed value is returned. So if want your subroutine to always return a true value by which I mention 1 (one), it's better to end the subroutine by adding 1; before the braces.

This page is intentionally left blank

BASIC PERL PROGRAM

Consider the following script,

Script

```
print q/Also a string\n/; #Equivalent to ‘’

print        qq{\ngokul.amuthan.s\@gmail.com\n};
#Equivalent to “ ”

print 'MA' x 5;

print "\n";

$h="Hello";

$w="World\n";

print $h.$w;

@abc = ('a','b','c','d');

@cba = @abc x 5;

print @abc,"\n";

print join(',',@abc);

print "\n";

print join(',',@cba);

print "\n";

print "Array is ",@abc;

print "\n\$abc[1]=",$abc[1];

$[=1;

print "\nAfter \$[=1\n\$abc[1]=",$abc[1];
```

```
print "\n";

print rand 10;

print "\n";

print 1>=1;

print "\n";

print 10<=>10,"\t",10<=>20,"\t",30<=>20;

# depends on the left statement is numerically eg, le, ge to right side

print "\n";

$a=undef;

$a+=10;

print $a;

print "\n";

$b+=3;

print $b;

print "\n";

print 'a'=='b'
```

Output

```
G:\ Programs\Perl>perl p3.pl

Use of assignment to $[ is deprecated at p3.pl line 19.

Also string\n

gokul.amuthan.s@gmail.com

MAMAMAMAMA
```

```
Hello,World

abcd

a,b,c,d

44444

Array is abcd

$abc[1]=b

After $[=1

$abc[1]=a

2.04407536498369

1

0        -1       1

10

3

1
```

The above script contains example of variables, arrays and simple logical relational operators. The above is simple script which needs no lengthy explanation, but there are few new topics involved in them, which I will discuss now.

Firstly the x-repetition operator; what this does is it duplicates the strings x number of times. The syntax is **"string" x num**, then the string is appended 'num' number of times. If it is used with array then the length of the array is duplicated 'num' number of times. **$[** is a inbuilt variable in Perl, which alters the index of the array. (Note it's too dangerous to alter this variable).

The next new topic is **rand num**; which generates random number between 0 and 'num'. The value is always in real value (with decimal value).

Another new keyword is **undef** which is similar to NULL in C, if a variable is initialized with undef then the variable is said to be undefined. The comparison operator <=> takes two operands a, b such that a<=>b and return value 0, if a and b are same; -1, if a is less than b; 1, if a is greater than b. Also you would be curious that I have used q// and qq{} for ' ' and " "; it's because Perl supports numerous quoting operators. Instead of // we can use any other interpolation such as !! or [] or <> ... etc If you want to print any escape sequence characters a \ is preceded before them, for example to print @ in the string we must use as \@.

Script

```
@array=('a','b','c');

my $a=@array;

print
"\n",@array,"\n",join(',',@array),"\n",$a;

my @array2=(1..4,6,7);

my $b=@array2;

print
"\n",@array2,"\n",join(';',@array2),"\n",$b;

#Logical

print "\n";

print @array && @array2;

print "\n";
```

```
print "AND  ",'ab' && 'cd';
print "\n";
print "OR   ",'ab' || 'cd';
print "\n";
print "NOT  ",~'cdca';
print "\n";
#Bitwise
print "\n";
print "AND  ",'a' & 'b';
print "\n";
print "OR   ",'a' | 'b';
print "\n";
print "EXOR ",'a' ^ 'b';
print "\n";
print "NOT  ",!'cdca';
print "\n";
sleep 10;
```

Output

```
G:\ Programs\Perl>perl p4.pl
abc
a,b,c
3
123467
```

```
1;2;3;4;6;7

6

123467

AND   cd

OR    ab

NOT   £¢£₨


AND   `

OR    c

EXOR  _

NOT
```

In the above script, we see that there is a unique assignment, **$b=@array2;** which means the scalar variable $b is assigned with the length of the array list @array2, which is the number of elements in the list. At last the script ends with **sleep num**; which halts the execution for 'num' seconds. (We will see this in detail forthcoming chapter). Balance are sample execution for logical and bitwise logical operators, which is similar as in other languages. Note, that I have ignored the below statements for the above scripts, but the best practice is to use the below statements.

```
use 5.10.1;

strict;

use warnings;
```

READING INPUT FROM CONSOLE

Similar to other languages, Perl allows terminal reading of input. But in Perl it's very simple and no format strings are required as variable can hold any datatype. This may sound as an advantage but it adds an overhead to check which type is read, even though some are handled internally by Perl itself, for some case it leads to additional overhead. The syntax to read a value from terminal is **$var=<STDIN>;** The variable 'var' is stored with values unless an "\n" (new line) is encountered. The variable var contains "\n" along with it so when you print the var, "\n" is also printed.

Script

```
#Simple implementation

print "\nWithout chomp or chop\n";

print "Enter a name(15 char only)\t";

my $name=<STDIN>;

$name=(length($name)  <=  15)?("Hello,$name.How
are you?\n"):("Enter a smaller name\n");

print $name;

#chop implementation

print "\nWith chop\n";

print "Enter a name(15 char only)\t";

$name=<STDIN>;
```

```
chop $name;

$name=(length($name)  <=  15)?("Hello,$name.How are you?\n"):("Enter a smaller name\n");

print $name;

#chomp implementation

print "\nWith chomp\n";

print "Enter a name(15 char only)\t";

$name=<STDIN>;

chomp $name;

$name=(length($name)  <=  15)?("Hello,$name.How are you?\n"):("Enter a smaller name\n");

print $name;
```

Output

```
G:\Programs\Perl>perl p6.pl


Without chomp or chop

Enter a name(15 char only)      Gokul

Hello,Gokul

.How are you?


With chop

Enter a name(15 char only)      Amuthan

Hello,Amuthan.How are you?
```

```
With chomp

Enter a name(15 char only)      Gokul Amuthan

Hello,Gokul Amuthan.How are you?
```

Chomp and chop function:

Chop removes the last character blindly, whereas chomp removes the last character if it matches with $/ (which is new line). $/ is a special variable used by Perl. User cannot alter it as it leads to warnings or a deprecation error in newer versions. The previous script clearly explain the functionality of chop and chomp. So what to go with either chop or chomp? It up with user to decide, but note that chomp is safer version in removing newline character while reading from terminals.

The syntax is **chop $var** and **chomp $var,** if $var is not specified then $_ is taken as default variable. Note $_ is a special variable in Perl which denotes the default input. If no specific variable is specified for some function and operators then $_ takes the default input space.

Script

```
#chmop function

print "\n chomp function\n";

my $a="abcde\n\t";

print 'abcde\n\t',"\t",length($a);

chomp $a;

print "\t",length($a),"\n";
```

```
$a="abcde\t\n";
print 'abcde\t\n',"\t",length($a);
chomp $a;
print "\t",length($a),"\n";
#chop function
print " chop function\n";
$a="abcde\n\t";
print 'abcde\n\t',"\t",length($a);
chop $a;
print "\t",length($a),"\n";
$a="abcde\t\n";
print 'abcde\t\n',"\t",length($a);
chop $a;
print "\t",length($a),"\n";
```

Output

```
G:\ Programs\Perl>perl p5.pl
 chomp function
abcde\n\t       7       7
abcde\t\n       7       6
 chop function
abcde\n\t       7       6
abcde\t\n       7       6
```

MULTIPLE ASSIGNMENTS

Multiple assignments are allowed in Perl that is in a single line we can do multiple value assignments to multiple variable. For example, consider the script

Script

```
#multiple assignment in a single statement

my ($a,$b)=(1,'a');

print "\n$a\t$b";

my ($c,@array)=('g',3..9,11,21);

#Is same as my ($c,@array) =
('g',(3..9,11,21));

print "\n$c\t",join(',',@array);

my ($a,$b,$c)=('f',33.4,43);

print "\n$a\t$b\t$c";
```

Output

```
G:\ Programs\Perl>perl p7.pl


1       a

g       3,4,5,6,7,8,9,11,21

f       33.4    43
```

The above script shows various multiple assignments, this not the restriction, you can perform various form as you wish but keep in mind not to assign the array list first then to scalar that is **(@a, $b)** should be avoided because Perl gets confused how much to assign to array and what value to scalar, so what Perl does is it assign entire thing to array and scalar is left unassigned. So what about hashes I would leave that for reader to work out. But I give a hint here, Perl would use alternate elements as key and data to store in hash. If an extra data is available it lead to imbalance.

The concept of multiple assignments work differently for different types of variables. So to be familiar with it, you should work out with more examples.

Try the following:

1) (%h, @a)
2) (%h, $a)
3) (%h, %h)
4) (@a, @b)

SOME SPECIAL FEATURES

Length function: To find the length of the parameter passed if no parameter then $_ is taken. The syntax is **length EXPR.** EXPR can be a scalar or list.

Join function: Printing list can be messier, writing a code to print the list is again an overhead and so Perl offers an inbuilt function that will separate the list item by the user specified character. The syntax is **join (list_separator, list).** The list_separator can be any string and list can be an array or hash.

Sort function: Sorting is again an overhead to code which can be reduced by using this function. It always sorts in ascending order. The syntax is **sort LIST**. To obtain descending order there is another function called **reverse** and the syntax is **reverse LIST**. To directly obtain the reverse sorted list user can combine both function and perform the operation.

Script

```
#Hashing list

%hash=('Apple' =>20,'Orange' =>15,'Banana'
=>5,'Strawberry' =>25);

print "\n",join ('-',%hash);

print "\n\$hash{'Apple'}=",$hash{'Apple'};

print "\n%hash{'Apple'}=",%hash{'Apple'};

#Sorting Hash items

print "\n\nSorting the hash
list\n",join(';',sort(%hash));
```

```
print "\n\nReverse Sorting the hash
list\n",join(';',reverse sort(%hash));
```

Output

```
G:\ Programs\Perl>perl p8.pl


Banana-5-Orange-15-Apple-20-Strawberry-25

$hash{'Apple'}=20

%hash{'Apple'}=Apple20


Sorting the hash list

15;20;25;5;Apple;Banana;Orange;Strawberry


Reverse Sorting the hash list

Strawberry;Orange;Banana;Apple;5;25;20;15
```

Note that I have use parenthesis in sort function but I haven't mentioned in syntax it's because Perl allows both styles.

Time function: To get time this function is used. This returns number of seconds since the epoch (00:00:00 UTC, January 1, 1970 for most system). There are three function that can be used,

$var=time;

($second, $minute, $hour, $date, $weekday, $year, $year_day, $daylight)=localtime;

($second, $minute, $hour, $date, $weekday, $year, $year_day, $daylight)=gmtime;

$timestr=localtime(time);

$year does not print exact year but to print exact year $year+1970 can be used. Each of the method is unique and prints different format. Both gmtime and localtime function are different in way they display value. The function localtime prints the time in your local area whereas gmtime prints the GMT time.

Script

```
#Selecting the list elements from function calls

($s,$m,$h)=(localtime())[0..2];

print "$h:$m:$s";

print "\n";

($d,$m,$y)=(localtime())[3..5];

print "$d/$m/$y";
```

Output

```
G:\ Programs\Perl>perl p33.pl

15:50:9

18/11/115
```

Script

```
#Ambiguity in this form

($s,$m,$h,$day,$month,$year,$w,$y,$is)=localtim
e(time);

print($s,"\t",$m,"\t",$h,"\t",$day,"\t",$month,
"\t",$year,"\t",$w,"\t",$y,"\t",$is);

#Correct result or less ambiguous form

$str=localtime(time);

print "\n",$str;
```

Output

```
G:\ Programs\Perl>perl p64.pl

3       51      15      18      11      115
5       351     0

Fri Dec 18 15:51:03 2015
```

Bare Words: The string initialized to a variable without any quotations are said to be bare words. Perl allows bare words, but it's not a good practice to do so. If the strict pragma is enabled then it results in warning.

Script

```
#use strict;

use warnings;

#Bare words

$msg=goodbye;

#Not a good use, give warning on run time if
strict pragma enabled
```

```
print "\n$msg";

$msg='goodbye';          #Good way to use

print "\n$msg";
```

Output

```
G:\ Programs\Perl>perl p9.pl

Unquoted string "goodbye" may clash with future
reserved word at p9.pl line 5.
```

goodbye

goodbye

Dynamicity of List: Lists can be dynamically created and initialized there is no limitation of list size unless there avails no memory. The following script creates a dynamically growing list.

Script

```
#Merging two static list

@a1=(1...5);

@a2=(6..10);

@a3=(@a1,@a2);

print "\nMerging ",join(',',@a1)," and
",join(',',@a2),"\nNew list ",join(',',@a3);

#Initializing the list dynamically

print "\n\nEnter the no. of item in the
list\t";

$n=<STDIN>;
```

```
chomp $n;
print "\nEnter the numbers for list\n";
for(0..($n-1))
{
      $a=<STDIN>;
      chomp $a;
      @list=(@list,$a);
}
print "\nThe list contains ",join(';',@list);
```

Output

```
G:\ Programs\Perl>perl p12.pl


Merging 1,2,3,4,5 and 6,7,8,9,10
New list 1,2,3,4,5,6,7,8,9,10


Enter the no. of item in the list       5
Enter the numbers for list
1
21
321
4321
54321
The list contains 1;21;321;4321;54321
```

Script

```
sub sums
{
	$a=@_;
	$a--;
	$sum=0;
	for(0..$a)
	{
		$sum = $sum + $_[$_];
	}
	return $sum;
}
@a1=(1...100);
print "\nThe sum of ",join('+',@a1)," is ",sums
@a1;
@a1=(1..5);
print "\n\nThe sum of ",join('+',@a1)," is
",sums @a1;
print "\n\nEnter the start and end bound\n";
$l=<STDIN>;
$u=<STDIN>;
@a2=($l..$u);
print "\nThe sum of ",join('+',@a2)," is ",sums
@a2;
```

Output

```
The sum of
1+2+3+4+5+6+7+8+9+10+11+12+13+14+15+16+17+18+19
+20+21+22+23+24+25+26+27+28+29+30+31+32+33+34+3
5+36+37+38+39+40+41+42+43+44+45+46+47+48+49+50+
51+52+53+54+55+56+57+58+59+60+61+62+63+64+65+66
+67+68+69+70+71+72+73+74+75+76+77+78+79+80+81+8
2+83+84+85+86+87+88+89+90+91+92+93+94+95+96+97+
98+99+100 is 5050


The sum of 1+2+3+4+5 is 15


Enter the start and end bound
4
15


The sum of 4+5+6+7+8+9+10+11+12+13+14+15 is 114
```

Upper and Lower Case: An additional feature of Perl is that it allows to modify the string case using escape sequences, rather than using functions to do so.

\u - Forces next character to be in upper case

\U - Forces the entire string to be in upper case until \E encountered

\l - Forces next character to be in lower case

\L - Forces the entire string to be in lower case until \E encountered

There is another escape sequence \E indicates that up to this the string case must be changed.

Script

```
print "\n\uhello";

print "\n\Uhello";

print "\n\lHELLO";

print "\n\LHELLO";

print "\n\Uhello w\Eorld";
```

Output

```
G:\ Programs\Perl>perl p13.pl


Hello

HELLO

hELLO

hello

HELLO World
```

Quoting Styles: As I have mentioned in earlier part of this book, we have the rights to change the quoting style. See the following example for better understanding.

Script

```
#Quoting styles
```

```
$msg=q/student's\n/;    #q// is similar to ''

print $msg;

$msg=qq/student's\n/;   #qq// is similar to ""

print $msg;

$msg=qq*She said "I can do this"\n*;

#qq** or qq{} or qq[] or qq!! or qq<> is
similar to ""

print $msg;
```

Output

```
G:\ Programs\Perl>perl p14.pl

student's\nstudent's

She said "I can do this"
```

Delimiter Interpolation: Again this is a most fabulous feature of Perl, which allows strings to continue to next line without making the string treated as separate lines. The following script demonstrates this feature clearly.

Script

```
#multi-line strings

$msg="This

is a

multi-line string"; # this is messy

print $msg,"\n\n";

#Delimiter interpolation

print <<EOF;
```

```
The string

starts

here

and ends here.\n\n

EOF

print <<"EOF";

This is again

a multi-lined

string. But with interpolations

\n

EOF

print <<'';

This

is

another way\n


#Previous blank line is necessary because ‘’
matches the next new line

print "This is another statement\n";

print <<""x 2;

\nThis is going to

be repeated

2 times..\n
```

Output

```
G:\ Programs\Perl>perl p16.pl
This
is a
multi-line string

The string
starts
here
and ends here.

This is again
a multi-lined
string. But with interpolations

This
is
another way\n
This is another statement
This is going to
be repeated
2 times..
```

```
This is going to
be repeated
2 times..
```

Script

```
print <<"EOFA","\n", <<"EOFB";
This is the first line and belongs to EOFA...
EOFA
This is the second line and belongs to EOFB...
EOFB
print "\n";
print <<'BL';
"Finished!"
BL
print "\n";
```

Output

```
G:\ Programs\Perl>perl p17.pl
This is the first line and belongs to EOFA...

This is the second line and belongs to EOFB...

"Finished!"
```

Revisiting Array: We already know that array can contain multiple datatype values but does array also support quoting style and you guessed it, arrays support quoting style. Let us see an example.

Script

```
#Arrays and lists

@a1=(1,2,'Hello',3.3,0b0000_1111);

print join('~',@a1);

print "\n";

#Avoid this

@a2=[3,'Hello',4];      # don't use square
brackets []

print @a2;

print "\n";

#qw// is similar to ()

@a3=qw/Mon Tues Wed Thurs Fri Sat Sun/;

print join(',',@a3);
```

Output

```
G:\Programs\Perl>perl p19.pl

1~2~Hello~3.3~15

ARRAY(0x2304e48)

        Mon,Tues,Wed,Thurs,Fri,Sat,Sun
```

ARRAY ACCESS

Perl offers another great feature to access array that is using negative values to access the data. Now that is pretty cool, because most of time when we calculate our index in negative it would be added advantage. Since negative value are started from reverse this might add slight confusion to novice learners. But once you get the hang of it, you can able to realize how easy it will be to access a data. A good sample code can explain this concept.

Script

```
#Extracting and Numbering

#Indices numbering

#Forward  0  1  2  3  4  5  6

#Backward-7 -6 -5 -4 -3 -2 -1

@array =( 1, 2, 3, 4, 5, 6, 7);

print"\nThe    length    of    the    array    is
",scalar(@array);

print "\n\nFirst element";

print "\n\$array[0]  ",$array[0];

print "\n\$array[-7]  ",$array[-7];

print "\n\nLast element";

print "\n\$array[6]  ",$array[6];

print "\n\$array[-1]  ",$array[-1];
```

Output

```
G:\ Programs\Perl>perl p20.pl

The length of the array is 7

First element
$array[0]  1
$array[-7]  1

Last element
$array[6]  7
$array[-1]  7
```

Now that we know that Perl allows negative indices now, what happens to fractional indices, Perl just convert them implicitly to the required format automatically. But what happens while using a **sprintf** function. First let us see what this function does. The syntax of this function is

sprintf (FORMAT, LIST);

FORMAT is the formatting string and the list is set of variables. The sprintf takes the FORMAT to return a formatted string but it doesn't print it on console. Let us see a sample script that helps us to understand this function.

Script

```
#shifting the places and rounding off

print sprintf("%5.9f",(99/7));

print "\n";

printf("%6d",5);

print "\n";

printf("%.3d",5);
```

Output

```
G:\ Programs\Perl>perl p22.pl

14.142857143

     5

005
```

Now back to our index calculation, what happens when we use sprintf inside the index calculation. Same Perl would implicitly convert it, then is there a difference between those, and yes there is. This difference is due to the format string we are going to use. See the following script that explains this muddle.

Script

```
#Calculating bound

@array=(1,2,3,4,5);

print "\narray[13/7] (int) is ",$array[13/7];

print "\narray[13/7] (float) is ",
$array[sprintf("%1.0f",(13/7))], "\n";
```

Output

```
G:\ Programs\Perl>perl p21.pl


array[13/7] (int) is 2

array[13/7] (float) is 3
```

Maximum size of Array: The maximum array size can be obtained using scalar function but what about the max index possible. Obviously any programmer would know the max index possible is ARRAY_SIZE-1 but Perl offers another way to know the max index using $#.

Script

```
#Sizes of array

@a=(1...30);

print "\n",join('-',@a);

print "\nThe size of array(scalar \@a)
:",scalar(@a);

print "\nThe max index of array(\$#a)  :",$#a;
```

Output

```
G:\ Programs\Perl>perl p24.pl


1-2-3-4-5-6-7-8-9-10-11-12-13-14-15-16-17-18-
19-20-21-22-23-24-25-26-27-28-29-30

The size of array(scalar @a) :30

The max index of array($#a)  :29
```

SLICING ARRAY

In certain cases, we are forced to split the array into some chunks, so now let us learn how to split the array to form new array. There are two methods that you can use,

1. Keeping array as it is and access using their index, but this one is kind of boring and simple.
2. Another way is to assign a set of required elements to a new array.

Now let us see this via a simple script.

Script

```
#Slicing array

@array=(0...10);

print "\@array=(0...10)
",join(',',@array);

@newarray=@array[3...7];

print "\@newarray=\@array[3...7]
",join(',',@newarray);

@newarray=@array[-5...-1];

print "\@newarray=\@array[-5...-1]
",join(',',@newarray);

print "\@array[1,2]
",join(';',@array[1,2]);
```

Output

```
G:\ Programs\Perl>perl p23.pl
@array=(0...10)  0,1,2,3,4,5,6,7,8,9,10
@newarray=@array[3...7]  3,4,5,6,7
@newarray=@array[-5...-1]  6,7,8,9,10
@array[1,2]   1;2
```

The newarray is the array that is formed by slicing the array by method two. Later in the book we will introduce another method called splicing.

HASHES

Hash is one of the beautiful data structure that emphasizes the feature of Perl. We already came across how to create a hash in Perl. Now let us see its striking features. Hashes can be considered as array list but added that it's formed with keys and respective values.

Script

```
#Hashes

%hash=('Mon'=>1, 'Tues'=>'2', 'Wed'=>3,
Thurs=>4, 'Fri'=>5, 'Sat'=>6, 'Sun'=>7);

print "\n";

print join('=',%hash);

#Extracting single and slices

print "\n\$hash{'Wed'}  ",$hash{'Wed'};

print "\n\$hash{Thurs}  ",$hash{Thurs};

print "\n\$hash{'Thurs'}  ",$hash{'Thurs'};

print "\n\n";

print "join(\"\\n\",\@hash{'Mon','Fri'})
",join("-",@hash{'Mon','Fri'});
```

Output

```
G:\ Programs\Perl>perl p25.pl


Thurs=4=Tues=2=Wed=3=Sun=7=Mon=1=Fri=5=Sat=6

$hash{'Wed'}  3
```

```
$hash{Thurs}  4

$hash{'Thurs'}  4


join("\n",@hash{'Mon','Fri'})   1-5
```

Keys and Values of Hash: There is also another way to retrieve the keys and values of hash data structure, which is by using **keys %HASH** and **values %HASH**. This returns an array containing the respective data.

Script

```
#Extracting keys and values

%hash=('Mon'=>1, 'Tues'=>'2', 'Wed'=>3,
Thurs=>4, 'Fri'=>5, 'Sat'=>6, 'Sun'=>7);

print "\nHashes values contain\n",join('-
>',values %hash);

print "\nHashes keys contain\n",join('->',keys
%hash);
```

Output

```
G:\ Programs\Perl>perl p26.pl


Hashes values contain

4->2->6->3->5->7->1

Hashes keys contain

Thurs->Tues->Sat->Wed->Fri->Sun->Mon
```

Also note that each time while printing your hash you may get different output after all it is what hash does.

Accessing Hash: The hash can be easily accessed using a special looping system call **for-each** loop. A for each loop will be discussed later for now let's see how it's used.

Script

```
#for each loop for extracting the hashes

%hash=('Mon'=>1, 'Tues'=>'2', 'Wed'=>3,
Thurs=>4, 'Fri'=>5, 'Sat'=>6, 'Sun'=>7);

foreach $k (%hash)

{

	if($hash{$k})

	{

		print "\n $k is the $hash{$k} day
of the week";

	}

}
```

Output

```
G:\ Programs\Perl>perl p27.pl

 Mon is the 1 day of the week

 Sun is the 7 day of the week

 Thurs is the 4 day of the week

 Wed is the 3 day of the week

 Tues is the 2 day of the week

 Fri is the 5 day of the week

 Sat is the 6 day of the week
```

Note that I have used if statement inside the loop it's because, for-each extracts all the data both keys and values from hash. And only the keys has values not the reverse that is, we cannot get keys from values. To block such condition it's used.

Another way of accessing the hash is to use the **each** function. This return a key and it's respective value. The syntax is **each %HASH**

Script

```
#Using each and while loop to extract the
hashes

%hash=('Mon'=>1, 'Tues'=>'2', 'Wed'=>3,
Thurs=>4, 'Fri'=>5, 'Sat'=>6, 'Sun'=>7);

while (($k, $v)= each %hash)

{

      print "\n$k=>$v";

}
```

Output

```
G:\ Programs\Perl>perl p28.pl


Thurs=>4

Sun=>7

Wed=>3

Tues=>2

Fri=>5
```

```
Mon=>1

Sat=>6
```

Sorting Hashes: Similar to array we can sort the hashes with the use of sort function. But simply passing hash will does not sort the keys and values separately. Additionally if you want them separately sorted then the **keys** or the **values** functions is used along with them.

Script

```
#Sorting the hashes

%hash=('Mon'=>1, 'Tues'=>'2', 'Wed'=>3, Thurs=>4, 'Fri'=>5, 'Sat'=>6, 'Sun'=>7);

print "\n\nSorting with keys\n",sort keys %hash;

print "\n\nSorting with values\n",sort values %hash;

print "\n\nSorting simply\n",sort %hash;
```

Output

```
G:\ Programs\Perl>perl p29.pl

Sorting with keys

FriMonSatSunThursTuesWed


Sorting with values

1234567
```

```
Sorting simply

1234567FriMonSatSunThursTuesWed
```

Existence of Hash value for a key: We can check whether a value exists for a key in hash using **exists EXPR** function. Already we saw that we can use in if statement but this is much safer.

Script

```
#checking for existence

%hash=('Mon'=>1,      'Tues'=>'2',      'Wed'=>3,
Thurs=>4, 'Fri'=>5, 'Sat'=>6, 'Sun'=>7);

print "Enter a week name\t";

$val=<STDIN>;

chomp $val;

if(exists($hash{$val}))

{

      print  "$val  is  $hash{$val}  day  of  the
week";

}

else

{

      print "Enter a valid week name";

}
```

Output

```
G:\ Programs\Perl>perl p30.pl

Enter a week name        Mon

Mon is 1 day of the week


G:\ Programs\Perl>perl p30.pl

Enter a week name        Jan

Enter a valid week name
```

We saw that the hash organize its data according to its wish so what is the way to guarantee the order of hash. Better option available is to sort the hash according to key or either by values. This does not affect the hash values of the keys. The following script demonstrates this.

Script

```
#Guarantee the order

%hash=('Mon'=>1,      'Tues'=>'2',      'Wed'=>3,
Thurs=>4, 'Fri'=>5, 'Sat'=>6, 'Sun'=>7);

print "\n",join('|',keys %hash);

@sorthash =sort keys %hash;

print "\n",join('|',@sorthash);

#Printing the hash

print "\nThe list contains\n";

foreach $k (@sorthash)
```

```
{
      print "$k->$hash{$k}\n";
}
#Size of the hash
print "\nThe size of the hash is";
print "\n(Keys) ",scalar keys %hash;
print "\n(Values) ",scalar values %hash;
```

Output

```
G:\ Programs\Perl>perl p31.pl
Fri|Wed|Tues|Thurs|Mon|Sun|Sat
Fri|Mon|Sat|Sun|Thurs|Tues|Wed
The list contains
Fri->5
Mon->1
Sat->6
Sun->7
Thurs->4
Tues->2
Wed->3

The size of the hash is
(Keys) 7
(Values) 7
```

Hash to Array List: A hash can be converted to list simply by initializing it to an array variable. And vice versa can be done from array to hash. During so it convert the first one to key and second to its respective value, if value is not enough then it results in undefined value.

Script

```
#Hash into List
%hash=('a'=>1,'b'=>2,'c'=>3);
print "Initial hash\n";
while(($k, $v)= each %hash)
{
      print "$k has $v\t";
}
@list=%hash;
print "\nHash to List\n";
print join(',',@list);
#List to Hash
%hash=@list;
print "\nList to Hash\n";
while(($k, $v)= each %hash)
{
      print "$k has $v\t";
}
```

Output

```
G:\ Programs\Perl>perl p35.pl
Initial hash
a has 1 c has 3 b has 2
Hash to List
a,1,c,3,b,2
List to Hash
a has 1 c has 3 b has 2
```

Script

```
#Hash into the scalar
%hash=(1..6);
($a,$b)=%hash;
print "$a  $b";
```

Output

```
G:\ Programs\Perl>perl p34.pl
5  6

G:\ Programs\Perl>perl p34.pl
3  4
```

TYPEGLOBS

Typeglobs are special type of variable which is nothing but a pointer to a symbol table entry. So what is a symbol table, it's a data structure maintained by a compiler or an interpreter to store all the variables defined in the script. This is a simple explanation to symbol table but it's a vast topic and you can understand by studying compiler design. The syntax of typeglobs is ***var**.

Script

```
#Typeglobs means "everything called"

sub sample

{

      my $sm='Hello';

      return *sm;

}

$n=100;

$a=*n;

print *STDOUT,"\n";

print *STDIN,"\n";

print $a,"\n";

print sample;
```

Output

```
G:\ Programs\Perl>perl p36.pl

*main::STDOUT

*main::STDIN

*main::n

*main::sm
```

The typeglobs are similar to pointer in C, but with a slight changes. Not to be confused with references which are actually the pointer type in Perl.

UNDEFINED VALUES

Sometime there are situation where we need to initialize a value but not a zero or any other number. In such cases Perl allows us to use a value called **undef** which is similar to NULL value.

Script

```
#Defined function - returns false if $variable
is undefined or has a undef value --> undefined
values

$val =undef;

if($val)

{

	print "Value is defined\n";

}

else

{

	print "Value is not defined\n";

}

$val=10;

if($val)

{

	print "Value is defined\n";

}

else
```

```
{
      print "Value is not defined\n";
}


$value=undef;
if(defined($value))
{
      print "Value defined\n";
}
else
{
      print "\$value may not exist or it must
have an undef value\n";
      $value=0;
}
$value=10;
if(defined($value))
{
      print "Value defined\n";
}
else
{
      print "\$value may not exist or it must
have an undef value\n";
```

```
    $value=0;
}
```

Output

```
G:\ Programs\Perl>perl p37.pl
Value is not defined
Value is defined
$value may not exist or it must have an undef value
Value defined
```

You can see that I have used a function called **defined**, its purpose is to check whether the variable is defined with a values or not. It returns true if variable is defined, else false is returned.

This page is intentionally left blank

SPECIAL TOKENS

There are some special Token in Perl which includes

__LINE__ which specifies the line number in the script, __FILE__ which denotes which script is being executed, __PACKAGE__ denoting which package is being executed, __END__ denoting the end of script.

Script

```
#Special Tokens of Perl

print "Current line is ",__LINE__,"\n";

print "Current File name is ",__FILE__,"\n";

print "Current Package name is
",__PACKAGE__,"\n";

#indicates the end of the script within a file
before the actual end of the file

__END__
```

Output

```
G:\ Programs\Perl>perl p38.pl

Current line is 2

Current File name is p38.pl

Current Package name is main
```

Script

```
package sample;

#Special Tokens of Perl

print "Current line is ",__LINE__,"\n";

print "Current File name is ",__FILE__,"\n";

print "Current Package name is
",__PACKAGE__,"\n";


package main;

print "Current Package name is
",__PACKAGE__,"\n";

#indicates the end of the script within a file
before the actual end of the file

__END__
```

Output

```
G:\ Programs\Perl>perl p38a.pl

Current line is 3

Current File name is p38a.pl

Current Package name is sample

Current Package name is main
```

CODE BLOCKS AND STATEMENTS

Code blocks or simply Blocks are sequence of statements. A block can be your entire script but most commonly we refer a set of statements enclosed within braces {}. Each block have its own scope. Any variable defined in a block lives only in that blocks scope. We can alter the sequence of execution to whether execute a block or execute them for some repeated number of times, with the following types of statements.

1) Conditional Statements
2) Looping Statements

Conditional Statements: The conditional statements can be used to alter the flow or make a block to execute or not based on certain condition. Perl allows two conditional statements, they are

1) If Else statement
2) Unless statement

Looping Statements: The loops allows us to execute a block to a specific number of iterations. Perl allows the following loops,

1) While loop
2) Do while loop
3) For loop
4) For-each loop

The conditional statements are useful when there are cases where the set of code has to be executed upon satisfying the condition. The if statements are same as in C. But Perl, as I have said before follows 'TIMTOWTDI' principle, has another statement called unless which is negation of if, that is if the condition fails then unless blocks execute. Why unless? There are some cases where failed condition has to be checked such example is in file reading where the reading has to be continued unless 'EOF' end of file is encountered.

The use of looping has proved to be quite useful when the first high level language was written. It avoids repeating your code over and over. If you are familiar with C, then there is no problem in understanding the first three types. The addition one is for-each loop which are most useful when you are dealing with array and hashes. The syntax of which you will see in further part of this book. Also loops can also be labelled through which we can allow certain code to be executed again or skipped.

IF STATEMENTS

If statements are most widely used statement for checking. There are several forms of if statements, the following shows syntax of if statements,

if (EXPR) { BLOCK }

if (EXPR) { BLOCK } else { BLOCK }

if (EXPR) { BLOCK } elsif (EXPR) { BLOCK } else { BLOCK }

STATEMENT if (EXPR);

STATEMENT is a single line operation whereas BLOCK is a collection of STATEMENTs.

Script

```
#if blocks

$a=15;

#Simple if

if($a==15)

{     print "\nValue is $a";   }


#Alternate way of simple if

print "\nStatement is printed" if ($a==15);

print "\nStatement is not printed" if($a!=15);


#If...else

if($a==10)
```

```
{     print "\nValue is 10";  }
else
{     print "\nValue is not 10";    }

#Else if
if($a<15)
{     print "\n$a is less than 15"; }
elsif($a>15)
{     print "\n$a is greater than 15";    }
elsif($a==15)
{     print "\nValue is $a";  }
else
{     print "\nSome other value";   }
```

Output

```
G:\ Programs\Perl>perl p40.pl


Value is 15
Statement is printed
Value is not 10
Value is 15
```

UNLESS STATEMENTS

A new type of conditional statement added in Perl, unless is a contradictory form of if statements. But there are no keywords like elsunless, we have to use elsif only to those parts.

unless (EXPR) { BLOCK }

unless (EXPR) { BLOCK } else { BLOCK }

unless (EXPR) { BLOCK } elsif (EXPR) { BLOCK } else { BLOCK }

STATEMENT unless (EXPR);

STATEMENT is a single line operation whereas BLOCK is a collection of STATEMENTs.

Script

```
#unless blocks are similar to if blocks

#If the if has == then unless should have !=

$a=10;

print "$a is the value\n", unless($a!=10);


unless($a>10)

{     print "$a is greater than 10";       }

elsif($a<10)

{     print "$a is less than 10";   }

elsif($a==10)
```

```
{     print "$a is equal to 10";    }
else
{     print "$a is some other value";     }
```

Output

```
G:\ Programs\Perl>perl p41.pl
10 is the value
10 is greater than 10
```

Conditional operator: A simple way of emulating if...else is by using conditional operator. The syntax is **(condition)?True_Statement:False_Statement;**

Script

```
#Conditional operator
$a=10;
($a==10)? print "\$a is 10":print "\$a is not 10";
```

Output

```
G:\ Programs\Perl>perl p42.pl
$a is 10
```

LOOPING STATEMENTS

Loops allows us to achieve DRY (Don't Repeat Yourself) scripts. All the basic looping system allowed in C is allowed in Perl. Added that it allows a new kind of loop called for-each loop. The syntax of each looping is,

while (EXPR) { BLOCK }

while (EXPR) { BLOCK } continue { BLOCK }

STATEMENT while (EXPR);

do { BLOCK } while (EXPR);

do { BLOCK } until (EXPR);

for (INITIALIZATION; CONDITION; INCREMENT/DECREMENT) { BLOCK }

for($initial_value..$final_value) { BLOCK }

for (INITIALIZATION; CONDITION; INCREMENT/DECREMENT) { BLOCK } continue { BLOCK }

foreach VAR (LIST) { BLOCK }

Script

```
#while and do..while Looping Statements

$a=5;

print "Single line while loop\n";

print $a--," " while($a>=0);


print "\nBlock while loop\n";
```

```
while($a<=5)
{
	print "$a ";
	$a++;
}

print "\nBlock do while loop\n";
do
{
	print "$a ";
	$a--;
}while ($a>=0);
```

Output

```
G:\ Programs\Perl>perl p43.pl
Single line while loop
5 4 3 2 1 0
Block while loop
-1 0 1 2 3 4 5
Block do while loop
6 5 4 3 2 1 0
```

While loop is called the entry controlled loop cause it allows to execute code only when the condition satisfies.

Whereas the do...while loop is called an exit check loop and allow to execute code at least once.

Like unless in conditional statements, to compensate that in looping we have do...until loop. See the below script to understand the difference.

Script

```
#until Looping statements

#inverse of do.. while


print "do..until loop\n";

$a=5;

do

{

	print $a," ";

	$a--;

}until $a>=0;


print "\ndo..while loop\n";

$a=5;

do

{

	print $a," ";

	$a--;
```

```
}while $a>=0;
```

Output

```
G:\ Programs\Perl>perl p44.pl
do..until loop
5
do..while loop
5 4 3 2 1 0
```

Script

```
#for and foreach Looping statements
for($i=0;$i<5;$i++)
{
	print "H ";
}
print "\n";

%h=('a'=>1,'b'=>2,'c'=>3,'d'=>4);
foreach $k (%h)
{
	if($h{$k})
	{
		print "$k->$h{$k}\t";
	}
}
```

```
print "\n";


@a= values %h;
foreach (@a)
{
      print $_,"\t";
}
```

Output

```
G:\ Programs\Perl>perl p45.pl
H H H H H
d->4    c->3    b->2    a->1
4       3       2       1
```

Script

```
#continue blocks
$i=10;
$sum=0;
while ($i>0)
{
      $sum=$sum+$i;
      print "w ";
}
continue
{
```

```
        $i--;
        print "c\t";
}
print "\nThe sum of 1 to 10 is $sum";
```

Output

```
G:\ Programs\Perl>perl p46.pl
w c       w c       w c       w c       w c       w c
w c     w c     w c     w c
The sum of 1 to 10 is 55
```

Labeling the loop: Sometime labelling a loop is quite useful to understand the purpose of the loop in script. But using comments are tend to be more convenient. But apart from it, we can use it to alter the flow of control by using the **goto** statement.

goto LABEL; - The control automatically shifts to the statements under the label LABEL.

redo LABEL; - It restarts the current loop and no further statements in block are executed.

next LABEL; - It causes the current loop iteration to skip to the next value.

last LABEL; - It causes the current iteration to be last iteration even there exist some further iterations.

Script

```
#Labelling
print "Enter the count\n";
$c=<STDIN>;
chomp $c;
SLEEP: for($i=0;$i<5;$i++)
{
	sleep 1;
	print "\nSleeping..";
}
if($c!=0)
{
	$c--;
	goto SLEEP;
}
print "\n\n\nBye...!!";
```

Output

```
G:\ Programs\Perl>perl p47.pl
Enter the count
1


Sleeping..
Sleeping..
```

```
Sleeping..
Sleeping..
Sleeping..
Sleeping..
Sleeping..
Sleeping..
Sleeping..
Sleeping..


Bye...!!
```

Script

```
#Loop controlling - next
$i=0;
while($i<=10)
{
	$i++;
	print "Entry ";
	if ($i==5)
	{
		print "Skipped\n";
		next;
	}
```

```
        print "$i\n";
}
```

Output

```
G:\ Programs\Perl>perl p48.pl
Entry 1
Entry 2
Entry 3
Entry 4
Entry Skipped
Entry 6
Entry 7
Entry 8
Entry 9
Entry 10
Entry 11
```

Script

```
#Loop controlling - last
$i=0;
while($i<=10)
{
        $i++;
        print "Entry ";
        if ($i==5)
```

```
        {
                print "Skipped entirely\n";
                last;
        }
        print "$i\n";
}
```

Output

```
G:\ Programs\Perl>perl p49.pl
Entry 1
Entry 2
Entry 3
Entry 4
Entry Skipped entirely
```

Script

```
#Loop controlling - last
$i=0;
while($i<=10)
{
        $i++;
        print "Entry ";
        if ($i==5)
        {
                print "Redoing the work\n";
```

```
                redo;
        }
        print "$i\n";
}
```

Output

```
G:\ Programs\Perl>perl p50.pl
Entry 1
Entry 2
Entry 3
Entry 4
Entry Redoing the work
Entry 6
Entry 7
Entry 8
Entry 9
Entry 10
Entry 11
```

Script

```
if(1)
{
        {
```

```
                last if(0);
                print "Really valid 1\n";
        }
        print "End 1\n";
}
if(1)
{
        {
                last if(1);
                print "Really valid 2\n";
        }
        print "End 2\n";
}
```

Output

```
G:\ Programs\Perl>perl p51.pl
Really valid 1
End 1
End 2
```

REVISITING SUBROUTINES

Already we saw how to define a subroutine and how to return values and pass parameter to them. Now we will see some added features that Perl supports.

Implicit variables: The $_ and @_ are implicit variable that can be used to access the parameters of subroutine. To access the elements in @_ we use $_[1], $_[2]... similar to normal array access but the name of the array is _ that is the difference. Now there must be question that you would be wanting to raise. Where to use $_ and where to use @_? The solution is, it is user's choice in code. Actually What Perl does is, it treats the parameters passed to the subroutine as an array list rather than as an individual element. So when to use $_ only, again it is user's wish, if he or she is confirm with the parameter length the $_ can be approached.

Script

```
#Subroutines

sub add

{

	$result=$_[0] + $_[1];

	print "The result is $result\n";

}

add(1,2);

add(4,9);
```

Output

```
G:\ Programs\Perl>perl p52.pl
The result is 3
The result is 13
```

Script

```
#Subroutines
sub ssort
{
	return join(',',sort(@_));
}

print ssort((1...9),(1,2,4),(-9...6));
#Perl merges all in to single array
```

Output

G:\ Programs\Perl>perl p53.pl

-1,-2,-3,-4,-5,-6,-7,-8,-9,0,1,1,1,2,2,2,3,3,4,4,4,5,5,6,6,7,8,9

Retrieving parameters separately: We learnt that Perl merges the entire parameter as a single array. But how to retrieve them to separate variable? Accessing array is too clumsy and make our script more complicated. This can be avoided by using a function called as **shift.** This function retrieves the first element of the array and store it to a variable.

shift @array;

shift; #takes the @_ variable by default

<u>Script</u>

```
#Shift function
#returns the first element of the list
sub sum
{
	my $r;
	while(@_)
	{
		$r+=shift;
	}
	return $r;
}
print sum(1,3),"\n";
print sum(1...10),"\n\n";
```

<u>Output</u>

```
G:\ Programs\Perl>perl p54.pl
4
55
```

See how the function **shift** can add dynamicity to the parameter passed. The ellipsis notation (...) allows to fill the values in-between.

Script

```
#Counting and Extracting arguments
sub extract
{
	if(@_==1)
	{
		my $d=@_;
		print "$d is the date\n";
	}
	elsif(@_==2)
	{
		my ($d,$m)=@_;
		print "$d day in $m month\n";
	}
	elsif(@_==3)
	{
		my ($d,$m,$y)=@_;
		print "$d day in $m month of $y year\n";
	}
	else
	{
		warn "Not enought arguments";
```

```
	}
}
extract;
extract(12);
extract(12,'May');
extract(12,"May",2015);
```

Output

```
G:\ Programs\Perl>perl p55.pl
Not enought arguments at p55.pl line 21.
1 is the date
12 day in May month
12 day in May month of 2015 year
```

Script

```
#Warning shift operation removes the first
element
my $sum;
@a=(1..5);
print join("\n",@a);
while(@a)
{
	$sum+=shift @a;
}
print "\nSum is $sum";
```

```
print "\nAfter shift array has ",join("\n",@a);
```

Output

```
G:\ Programs\Perl>perl p56.pl
1
2
3
4
5
Sum is 15
After shift array has
```

See after the shift operation when we tried to print the array, it prints nothing. So while using shift you must be careful not to alter the original copy rather make a duplicate then alter it.

Script

```
#passing array as argument
#Perl combines two or more array into a single array @_
sub arr
{
	my (@a,@b)=@_;
	print "Extract array A ",join(',',@a);
	print "\nExtract array B ",join(';',@b);
```

```
}

@a=(1..3);
@b=(4..9);
arr(@a,@b);
```

Output

```
G:\ Programs\Perl>perl p57.pl
Extract array A 1,2,3,4,5,6,7,8,9
Extract array B
```

When we try to pass two array to the subroutine again tragedy happens, that is Perl combines them into a single array and when we try to extract it will be failure. This is what happened in the previous script.

Passing hashes to subroutine: We already discussed that while a hash is passed to the subroutine it is implicitly converted to a list. So how to use it as a hash in subroutine? It's simple, yes you guessed it – assign that array to hash. We will see a simple code to demonstrate this. But what happens when a hash is passed along with an array, then it's a tragedy. So better not to pass a hash along with array. It's not that it's impossible, rather it increases to complexity of the code more.

Script

```
#passing Hashes
#Perl will convert them into list
#No such %_ will work
sub disp
{
	my %hash=@_;
	foreach (%hash)
	{
		print "$_ => $hash{$_}\n" if($hash{$_});
	}
}

%h=('a'=>1,'b'=>2,'c'=>3);
disp %h;
```

Output

```
G:\ Programs\Perl>perl p58.pl
a => 1
b => 2
c => 3
```

Script

```
#Comparing strings
#passing array/hash with scalar;
sub multi
{
	($a,@ar)=@_;
	if($a eq "add")		#Note	use	eq
operator than ==
	{
		my $sum;
		while(@ar)
		{
			$sum+=shift @ar;
		}
		print "\nSum is $sum";
	}
	elsif($a eq "sort")
	{
		print "\n",join(',',sort @ar);
	}
	else
	{
		print "\nEnter a valid option";
```

```
    }
}
multi("add",9,0,3,2,1);
@a=(4,2,5,8,1,9);
multi("sort",@a);
multi(@a);
```

Output

```
G:\ Programs\Perl>perl p59.pl


Sum is 15
1,2,4,5,8,9
Enter a valid option
```

Assigning default values: Some time there occurs a case where an undefined value can be returned by a subroutine, which is quite not desirable. So we assign a default value to those returning variables, so that this situation can be recovered. For these purpose we use || operator. Again it's just a programmer's concept. It's not mandatory to assign default values.

Script

```
#default values
sub powerOf
{
```

```
    my $base_val=shift || 1;
    my $power_val=shift || 1;
    return $base_val ** $power_val;
}
print "\npower(2,2)=",powerOf(2,2);
print "\npower()=",powerOf();
print "\npower(4,3)=",powerOf(4,3);
```

Output

```
G:\ Programs\Perl>perl p61.pl


power(2,2)=4
power()=1
power(4,3)=64
```

Dynamicity of Arguments: Argument can be made dynamic when we apply default values to our script. See the below code to understand the dynamicity more clearly.

Script

```
#Dynamic arguments
#Use hash to achieve this
sub powerOf
{
```

```
        my %arg=@_;
        if(scalar keys %arg <=2)
        {
              my $base_val=$arg{'b'}|| 1;
              my $power_val=$arg{'p'}||1;
              return $base_val ** $power_val;
        }
        else
        {
              return "Too many arguments";
        }
}

print        "\npowerOf('b'=>2,'p'=>3)         =
",powerOf('b'=>2,'p'=>3);
print         "\npowerOf('b',2,'p',3)          =
",powerOf('b',2,'p',3);
print "\npowerOf('b'=>2) = ",powerOf('b'=>2);
print "\npowerOf('p'=>3) = ",powerOf('p'=>3);
print "\npowerOf() = ",powerOf();
```

Output

```
G:\ Programs\Perl>perl p62.pl

powerOf('b'=>2,'p'=>3) = 8
powerOf('b',2,'p',3) = 8
powerOf('b'=>2) = 2
powerOf('p'=>3) = 1
powerOf() = 1
```

Ambiguous Returns: In some cases we are forced to return array and in some a scalar. So how to decide what the user wants and that to processed dynamically? There is two solution to this ambiguity,

1. Use of **wantarray** function.
2. Using scalar keyword.

Let us discuss the first method now. The **wantarray** is an inbuilt function of Perl which decides dynamically by analyzing the script and returns value 0 if scalar is expected and 1 if array is expected. There is no parameters for this function. The aliter approach is to use scalar keyword in front of the subroutine call.

Script

```
#Removing Context Ambiguity
#return as array or scalar
```

```
#Method 1
#wantarray() function
sub how
{
	if(wantarray)
	{
		return ('Array','Message',"\n");
	}
	else
	{
		return "Scalar Message\n";
	}
}
$scalarmsg=how();
$listmsg=join("--",how());
print $scalarmsg;
print $listmsg;

#Method 2
print "\n";
$s=scalar how;
print $s;
```

Output

```
G:\ Programs\Perl>perl p65.pl
Scalar Message
Array--Message--

Scalar Message
```

Attributes of method: Attributes of subroutine defines the nature of that subroutine. But it's not effectively utilized. Maybe in the forth-coming versions they can be of proper use. The attributes are:

lock - a lock obtained on subroutine before its executed

method - given method can't be resolved properly

lock method - ensures only one thread enter the execution of subroutine

lvalue - a subroutine can be used as a modifiable scalar value

They are used as

sub sub_name : attribute

{

#code block

}

Prototype of Subroutine: The prototype define the type or the form that the subroutine takes. This is useful to direct

Perl about the number of arguments and type of arguments to be passed.

Some of the sample prototypes are:

1. sub func ($) === func $var
2. sub func($$) === func $var1, $var2
3. sub func(@) === func @arr
4. sub func($@) == func $var, @arr === func $var, $a, $b, $c
5. sub func(\@$) == func @arr, $var
6. sub func($%) === func $var, %{$reference_of_hash}
7. sub func(\%$) === func %{$reference_of_hash}, $var
8. sub func(\@$$@) === func @arr1, $var1, $var2, @arr2
9. sub func(*$) === func HANDLE, $var1
10. sub func(*;@) === func HANDLE, @arr === func HANDLE
11. sub func(&$@) === func { #code } $var, @arr
12. sub func() === func

In the above twelve point the first defines the subroutine prototype, after which it defines the possible function call. Parameters after the semicolon in the prototype are said to be optional arguments.

Script

```
#Prototyping
sub display($$)
{
      print "Parameters ";
      print "\t",shift while(@_);
}
display 1,2;
```

Output

```
G:\ Programs\Perl>perl p67.pl
Parameters      1       2
```

Script

```
#Prototyping
sub display($@)
{
      print "\nScalar\t",shift;
      print "\nArray\t",@_;
}
my @a=(1,2,4,5,7,8);
$b=44.4;
display @a,@a;
print "\n";
display $b,@a;
```

```
print "\n";
display @a,$b;
print "\n";
display $b,$b;
print "\n";
display @a;
print "\n";
display $b;
```

Output

```
G:\ Programs\Perl>perl p68.pl


Scalar  6
Array   124578
Scalar  44.4
Array   124578
Scalar  6
Array   44.4
Scalar  44.4
Array   44.4
Scalar  6
Array
Scalar  44.4
Array
```

PACKAGES AND MODULES

The possible case where we define two subroutine of same name, but what Perl does it overwrites with most recent found code. If we want to have both the subroutines to be existing in our script then the only way is to define them in separate module. And import them to our script whenever they are required.

To define a package we use the keyword, **package**. If this is not specified in script then the default package is taken as **main** and all code is stored under it.

Script

```
package Sample;

sub calculate

{

            $a=shift;

            $b=shift;

            $c=shift;

            $res=$a+$c if($b eq '+');

            $res=$a-$c if($b eq '-');

            $res=$a*$c if($b eq '*');

            $res=$a/$c if($b eq '/');

      return $res;

}
```

```
package Sample2;
sub display
{
	print join(',',@_);
}

package main;
print "\n";
print Sample::calculate('1','+','2');
print "\n";
Sample2::display("Message","Hello");
```

Output

```
G:\ Programs\Perl>perl p69.pl


3
Message,Hello
```

In the above script we have written the packages in the same file. But that is not interesting and also if we want to use them in another script it's hard. So we now learn a way to write the module code separately from the main script. We call that file as **Perl Module**. These files are save with extension ".pm". Creating a module requires a bit of work in Perl and some rules have to be followed. It may look hard but once you understand why we are using each and every single line we can easily understand this concept. Now let's see the general structure.

#Creating Modules

package pack_name;

#Define package and module name

require Exporter;

#Import the functionality that are required to export subroutine from this module

@ISA = (Exporter);

#Initializing the inheritance tree so Perl can find this subroutine

@EXPORT = (func);

#Mention the subroutine that is to be exported

#The function definition of the subroutine that we want to export

sub func

{

#code;

}

1;

#Modules should return a true values

Now to use the defined module the following code is used.

use pack_name;

func();

It is as simple as that when you know why we write each piece of code rather than studying it as a syntax.

<u>Script</u>

Addition.pm

```
package Addition;

require Exporter;

@ISA = (Exporter);

@EXPORT = (add);

sub add

{

        my $a=0;

        $a+=shift while(@_);

        return $a;

}

1;
```

p74.pl

```
use Addition; #Addition.pm is a user defined package

print add(1,2);

print "\n";

print add(1,2,3,4,5);
```

Output

```
G:\ Programs\Perl>perl p74.pl

3

15
```

Other variables of Exporter: The exporter contains four variable in total, each with its own specialty. Now let us see each of them individually.

@EXPORT – Exports the default subroutines

@EXPORT_OK – Exports the subroutine if explicitly requested by the user

@EXPORT_FAIL – Restricts the user to export that specified subroutine. The alternate way is to put an underscore (_) before the name of the subroutine.

%EXPORT_TAGS – It's a hash that contains a set of importing sets.

Script

Perl\UserMath\Basic.pm

```
package Basic;

require Exporter;

@ISA=(Exporter);


#default

@EXPORT=(sum,diff,mul,div);
```

```
#If requested
@EXPORT_OK=(avg,nPr,nCr);
#Import sets
%EXPORT_TAGS=('std'=>[sum,diff,mul,div],

      'compute'=>[sum,diff,mul,div,nPr,nCr],

      'all'=>[sum,diff,mul,div,avg,nPr,nCr]);
#use _ before subroutine name to make the routine to be non-importable
#Or explicitly specify them in @EXPORT_FAIL array
@EXPORT_FAIL=(fact);
$_a=0;

sub sum(@)
{
      $_a+=shift while(@_);
      return $_a;
}

sub diff(@)
{
      $_a-=shift while(@_);
```

```
        return $_a;
}

sub mul(@)
{
        $_a=1;
        $_a*=shift while(@_);
        return $_a;
}

sub div(@)
{
        $_a=shift;
        $_a/=shift while(@_);
        return $_a;
}

sub avg(@)
{
        my $c=@_;
        my $a=sum(@_);
        return $a/$c;
}
```

```
sub nPr($$)
{
        my $n=shift;
        my $r=shift;
        my $nf=fact($n);
        my $nrf=fact($n-$r);
        return $nf/$nrf;
}

sub nCr($$)
{
        my $n=shift;
        my $r=shift;
        $n=nPr($n,$r);
        $r=fact($r);
        return $n/$r;
}

sub fact($)
{
        $_a=shift;
        if($_a==0 || $_a==1)
```

```
        {
                return 1;
        }
        my $f=1;
        while($_a>0)
        {
                $f*=$_a;
                $_a--;
        }
        return $f;
}
1;
```

Perl\UserMath\sample.pl

```
use Basic;
print
sum(2,2),"\n",diff(2,2),"\n",mul(2,2),"\n",div(
2,2);
```

Output

```
G:\ Programs\Perl\UserMath>perl sample.pl
4
0
4
1
```

Perl\UserMath\sample2.pl

```
use Basic "nPr";

print nPr(10,7);
```

Output

```
G:\ Programs\Perl\UserMath>perl sample2.pl

604800
```

Perl\UserMath\sample3.pl

```
use Basic "fact";

print fact 10;

#Will not execute
```

Output

```
G:\ Programs\Perl\UserMath>perl sample3.pl

"fact" is not exported by the Basic module

Can't continue after import errors at sample3.pl line 1.

BEGIN failed--compilation aborted at sample3.pl line 1.
```

Perl\UserMath\sample4.pl

```
use Basic ":all";

print avg(10,7);
```

Output

```
G:\ Programs\Perl\UserMath>perl sample4.pl
8.5
```

Perl\p75.pl

```
use UserMath::Basic ":all";
print Basic::nPr(10,7);
```

Output

```
G:\ Programs\Perl>perl p75.pl
604800
```

Require, Use, No keyword: The require statement searches the module in **@ISA**, whereas the use statement searches in **@EXPORT, @EXPORT_OK, %EXPORT_TAGS**. The no keyword, as the name says does not use that module in script after the current no statement and before the next use statement.

Script

```
require 'p65.pl';
```

Output

```
G:\ Programs\Perl>perl p76.pl
Scalar Message
Array--Message--
Scalar Message
```

Script

```
{
      my $a=10;;
}
no warnings;

print "\nAfter no statement";
print $a;

use warnings;

print "\nAfter use statement";
print $a;
```

Output

```
G:\ Programs\Perl>perl p79.pl

After no statement
Use of uninitialized value $a in print at p79.pl line 12.
After use statement
```

SPECIAL BLOCKS OF PERL

Apart from normal blocks, Perl allows four other special blocks that are useful to provide added control over the script. The four types are,

BEGIN block is executed during parsing process. **CHECK** block is executed as soon as parsing and compilation stages are completed. **INIT** block runs before the main flow of the script. **END** block executes on termination of the script. The flow of execution is **BEGIN->CHECK->INIT->Script->END.**

BEGIN and **INIT** executed in same order it's defined. **CHECK** and **END** executes last defined block first that is in reverse order. **BEGIN**, **CHECK**, **INIT** and **END** blocks are executed only once even if there are multiple process are running.

Script

```
if($pid=fork)
{
	print "\n\nProcess id = ",$pid,"\n";
	print "Child";
	sleep 1;
	goto label;
}
label:
print "\nMain Block 1";
```

```
CHECK
{	print "\nCheck 1";	}
END
{	print "\nEnd 1";	}
BEGIN
{	print "\nBegin 1";	}
INIT
{	print "\nInit 1"; }
END
{	print "\nEnd 2";	}
CHECK
{	print "\nCheck 2";	}
BEGIN
{	print "\nBegin 2";	}
INIT
{	print "\nInit 2"; }
print "\nMain Block 2\n";
```

Output

```
G:\Programs\Perl>perl p71.pl


Begin 1
Begin 2
Check 2
```

```
Check 1

Init 1

Init 2


Process id = -1204


Main Block 1

Main Block 2

Child

Main Block 1

Main Block 2


End 2

End 1
```

In the above script there is a line **$pid=fork** which is new statement that you have never crossed while reading this book. But if you know C language, then you must be able to recognize that **fork** is a system call that is used to create a child process. Here to it's used to create another process traditionally called as child process. We will discuss about process creation in forth-coming chapters.

Script

```
BEGIN

{     print "\nDuring Parsing process";    }

CHECK

{     print "\nAfter parsing and compilation
process";    }

INIT

{     print "\nBefore main flow of the script";
      }

print "\nMain script\n";

die "\nMain flow";

END

{     print "\nAfter the end of main flow and
before end of the script";    }
```

Output

```
G:\Programs\Perl>perl p72.pl


During Parsing process

After parsing and compilation process

Before main flow of the program

Main program

Main flow

After the end of main flow and before end of
the program
```

Usage of Special Blocks: Special blocks like BEGIN allows us to import module to our script before its execution rather than at execution. This is more useful to avoid handling errors due to missing modules.

Script

```
BEGIN
{
	require 'Addition.pm';
	Module->import();
}
print "add(4,5)=",Addition::add(4,5);
```

Output

```
G:\Programs\Perl>perl p77.pl
add(4,5)=9
```

Script

```
BEGIN
{
	use Addition;
}
print "add(4,5)=",add(4,5);
```

Output

```
G:\Programs\Perl>perl p78.pl
add(4,5)=9
```

Auto loading of subroutine using Special Blocks: When the name of the subroutine is given with a name **AUTOLOAD** then Perl automatically executes the subroutine placed in **$AUTOLOAD**. The **use subs** pragma is used to predeclare the subroutines that are going to be used. Hence by defining all possible name for the auto loading subroutine in the BEGIN block we can called them explicitly using those names. I know it's twisty to understand now, let us see a script to get a clear idea about it.

Script

```
#Auto loading
BEGIN
{
	$hash{"a"}=1;
	$hash{"b"}=2;
	$hash{"c"}=3;
}

use subs keys %hash;
print "Value of a is ",a;
```

```
print "Value of b is ",b;
print "Value of c is ",c;

sub AUTOLOAD
{
	my $con=$AUTOLOAD;
	print "\nBefore ",$con,"\n";
	$con=~s/.*:://;
	print "After ",$con,"\n";
	return $hash{"$con"};
}
```

Output

```
G:\Programs\Perl>perl p84.pl

Before main::a
After a
Value of a is 1
Before main::b
After b
Value of b is 2
Before main::c
After c
Value of c is 3
```

Note something unusual in the above script. $con=~s/.*:://// is called as regular expression. We will get to that later. For argument sake let's just know the meaning of that particular statement is alone. What it does is, it substitutes all the characters before '::' and also '::' by empty value, leaving characters after '::' to remain in the string. That is, if it is "**main::a**" then after that statement it would be "**a**" alone.

DATA MANIPULATION

Data is something that is raw whereas information is some structured format of collection of data. In different context different data has to be dealt with. To provide this Perl offers a great variety of functions to manipulate them as they are desired.

Script

```
use Math::Complex;

#Data manipulation

print "\nabs(-10.3243)=",abs(-10.3243);

print "\nint abs(-33.44)=",int abs(-33.44);

print "\nexp(2)=",exp(2);

print "\nsqrt(49)=",sqrt(49);

print "\nlog(44.64)=",log(44.64);

print "\nsin(30)=",sin(30);

print "\nsin(pi*30/180)=",sin(pi*30/180);

print "\nhex(\"CAFE44\")=",hex("CAFE44");

print "\noct(\"0xCAFE44\")=",oct("0xCAFE44");

print
"\noct(\"0b10001000\")=",oct("0b10001000");

print "\nchr(66)=",chr(66);

print "\nord('b')=",ord('b');

print "\nrand=",rand;

print "\nrand(10)=",rand(10);
```

```
print "\nsrand=",srand;
print "\nsrand(10)=",srand(10);
print "\ntime()=",time();
print "\n";
```

Output

```
G:\Programs\Perl>perl p86.pl
abs(-10.3243)=10.3243
int abs(-33.44)=33
exp(2)=7.38905609893065
sqrt(49)=7
log(44.64)=3.79863031807306
sin(30)=-0.988031624092862
sin(pi*30/180)=0.5
hex("CAFE44")=13303364
oct("0xCAFE44")=13303364
oct("0b10001000")=136
chr(66)=B
ord('b')=98
rand=0.431241387575032
rand(10)=7.38179660725535
srand=1918087972
srand(10)=10
time()=1450525267
```

The above script demonstrates the various possible way that the data can be manipulated using various function.

Packing the bits: There are some situation where the programmer is in need of a single bit, in such cases defining one variable for each bit is exhaustive use of memory. This disadvantage can be recovered by using **vec** function, which set the bit in the variable.

vec $VAR, position, bit_value

Script

```
#vec function

vec($bool,0,1)=0;

vec($bool,1,1)=1;

vec($bool,2,1)=0;

vec($bool,3,1)=0;

vec($bool,4,1)=0;

vec($bool,5,1)=0;

vec($bool,6,1)=1;

vec($bool,7,1)=0;

print length($bool);

print"\n",$bool;
```

Output

```
G:\Programs\Perl>perl p88.pl

1

B
```

Case Modification: Perl allows simple modification of cases using some predefined function such as,

lc $VAR – Changes the entire string to lower case.

lcfirst $VAR – Changes the first letter of the string to lower case.

uc $VAR – Changes the entire string to upper case.

ucfirst $VAR – Changes the first letter of the string to upper case.

Script

```
#Case modification

$str="The Bat sat and ate the rat\n";

print lc($str);

print lcfirst($str);

print uc($str);

print ucfirst($str);
```

Output

```
G:\Programs\Perl>perl p91.pl

the bat sat and ate the rat

the Bat sat and ate the rat

THE BAT SAT AND ATE THE RAT

The Bat sat and ate the rat
```

Position of the character or String: The position of the character or group of characters can be obtained by using the function **index** and **rindex**.

index $VAR, "Character" [,START_POSITION];

Returns position value of character from starting point of the string

rindex $VAR, "Character"[,START_POSITION];

Returns position value of character from end point of the string

The START_POSITION parameter is optional parameter and its specifies from where the search has to begin.

Script

```
#String location

#index searches the first occurrence of string

#rindex searches the last occurrence of string

$str="The Cat sat and ate the rat";

print "The string is \n\"$str\"\n";

print  "index(\$str,'cat')=",index($str,'cat');
print "\n";

print  "index(\$str,'Cat')=",index($str,'Cat');
print "\n";

print
"index(\$str,'Cat',4)=",index($str,'Cat',4);
print "\n";

print    "index(\$str,'at')=",index($str,'at');
print "\n";
```

```
print
"rindex(\$str,'cat')=",rindex($str,'cat');
print "\n";

print
"rindex(\$str,'Cat')=",rindex($str,'Cat');
print "\n";

print
"rindex(\$str,'Cat',4)=",rindex($str,'Cat',4);
print "\n";

print  "rindex(\$str,'at')=",rindex($str,'at');
print "\n";
```

Output

```
G:\Programs\Perl>perl p93.pl

The string is

"The Cat sat and ate the rat"

index($str,'cat')=-1

index($str,'Cat')=4

index($str,'Cat',4)=4

index($str,'at')=5

rindex($str,'cat')=-1

rindex($str,'Cat')=4

rindex($str,'Cat',4)=4

rindex($str,'at')=25
```

Fetching the substrings: Perl provides a facility to fetch substrings of a string for manipulation purpose. The **substr** function is used to perform this operation

substr $VAR, START_VAL[, OFFSET]

OFFSET value is optional. If it is not specified then the entire string after START_VAL is taken into consideration. Since Perl allows negative indexing the values can be negative. START_VAL value indicates from where the substring starts.

Note that we can use this technique to replace the substring by another.

Script

```
$str="0123456789";

print "\n\nThe string is $str\n\n";

print "\nsubstr(\$str,4)=",substr($str,4),"\n";

print
"\nsubstr(\$str,4,3)=",substr($str,4,3),"\n";

print        "\nsubstr(\$str,-7)=",substr($str,-
7),"\n";

print    "\nsubstr(\$str,4,-4)=",substr($str,4,-
4),"\n";

print      "\nsubstr(\$str,-4,4)=",substr($str,-
4,4),"\n";

print  "\nsubstr(\$str,-4,-2)=",substr($str,-4,-
2),"\n";
```

Output

```
G:\Programs\Perl>perl p94.pl

The string is 0123456789

substr($str,4)=456789

substr($str,4,3)=456

substr($str,-7)=3456789

substr($str,4,-4)=45

substr($str,-4,4)=6789

substr($str,-4,-2)=67
```

Script

```
#Replacing the value of string

$str="The Cat sat and ate the rat";

print "\nThe string is \"$str\"\n";

substr($str,4,3)="Lion";

print "The string after modification \"$str\"\n";

substr($str,4)="Lion";

print "The string after modification \"$str\"\n";
```

Output

```
G:\Programs\Perl>perl p95.pl

The string is "The Cat sat and ate the rat"
```

```
The string after modification "The Lion sat and ate the rat"

The string after modification "The Lion"
```

Splicing Array: Splicing means interweaving. This function takes two array and merges to a single array by replacing the specified set of elements.

splice @ARRAY1, $ARR1_START, $REPLACE_LENGTH, @ARRAY2

The @ARRAY2 elements are replaced in $ARR1_START position of @ARRAY1. If the length of the @ARRAY2 is less than the $REPLACE_LENGTH, in such cases the elements of @ARRAY1 are ignored. Also if @ARRAY2 is not specified then, the @ARRAY1 is replaced with empty list.

Script

```
@array=('a'...'g');

@array2=(1..4);

print "\nThe arrays are\n";

print join('-',@array);

print "\n",join(':',@array2);

print
"\n\nsplice(\@array,0,5,\@array2)\n",join('->',
splice(@array,0,5,@array2));

print "\nThe arrays are\n";

print join('-',@array);

print "\n",join(':',@array2);
```

```
print       "\n\nsplice(\@array,1,3)\n",join('-
',splice(@array,1,3));

print "\nThe arrays are\n";

print join('-',@array);

print "\n",join(':',@array2);

print       "\n\nsplice(\@array,2)\n",join('--
',splice(@array,2));

print "\nThe arrays are\n";

print join('-',@array);

print "\n",join(':',@array2);
```

Output

```
G:\Programs\Perl>perl p97.pl


The arrays are

a-b-c-d-e-f-g

1:2:3:4


splice(@array,0,5,@array2)

a->b->c->d->e

The arrays are

1-2-3-4-f-g

1:2:3:4


splice(@array,1,3)
```

```
2-3-4
The arrays are
1-f-g
1:2:3:4

splice(@array,2)
g
The arrays are
1-f
1:2:3:4
```

Formatting arrays: To display a list in the desired format is can require some piece of code which increases the number of lines of code. Instead Perl allows an inbuilt function to perform required formatting specified by the programmer. The syntax is **join FORMAT_EXPR, LIST**. List can be both array and hash, but while passing hash, it's internally converted to array format.

Another way is to use inbuilt list separator variable to perform this action. **$,** is initialized with the required format which is carried out internally by Perl.

Script

```
@arr=(1..5);
print "\nWithout join";
print "\n",@arr;
```

```
print "\nWith join";

print "\n",join('=',@arr);

print "\nWith \$,";

$,=';';

print "\n",@arr;
```

Output

```
G:\Programs\Perl>perl p98.pl


Without join

12345

With join

1=2=3=4=5

With $,

;1;2;3;4;5
```

Splitting the String: Sometime the string contains pieces of data separated by some separator. In such cases to extract those data, split function is used.

split /REG_EXPR/, EXPR, LENGTH_LIMIT

Script

```
$str="Hello How are you? I am fine What about you?";

print "\nsplit(/ /,\$str) ",split(/ /,$str);
```

```
print "\njoin('-',split(/ */,\$str)) ",join("-
",split(/ */,$str));

print "\nsplit(/ /,\$str,5) ",split(/
/,$str,5);

print "\njoin('-',split(/ /,\$str,5)) ",join("-
",split(/ /,$str,5));
```

Output

```
G:\Programs\Perl>perl p99.pl

split(/ /,$str)
HelloHowareyou?IamfineWhataboutyou?

join('-',split(/ */,$str)) H-e-l-l-o-H-o-w-a-r-
e-y-o-u-?-I-a-m-f-i-n-e-W-h-a-t-a-b-o-u-t-y-o-
u-?

split(/ /,$str,5) HelloHowareyou?I am fine What
about you?

join('-',split(/ /,$str,5)) Hello-How-are-you?-
I am fine What about you?
```

/ / means whitespaces are treated as separator. / */ means each character is treated as individual element. If LENGTH_LIMIT is specified the operation is carried out only of that many number of elements.

Script

```
#sorting using subroutine

@array=(1,9,2,8,3,7,4,6,5,0);

print "The array contains\n";
```

```
print join('-',@array);

print "\n\njoin('-',sort \@array)\n",join('-
',sort @array);

print "\n\njoin('-',sort {\$b cmp \$a}
\@array)\n",join('-',sort {$b cmp $a} @array);

print "\n\njoin('-',sort {\$a cmp \$b}
\@array)\n",join('-',sort {$a cmp $b} @array);

@array=('g','o','k','u','l','
','a','m','u','t','h','a','n','.','s');

print "\n\njoin('-',sort lex
\@array)\n",join('-',sort lex @array);

sub lex

{     $a cmp $b   }
```

Output

```
G:\Programs\Perl>perl p102.pl

The array contains

1-9-2-8-3-7-4-6-5-0

join('-',sort @array)

0-1-2-3-4-5-6-7-8-9

join('-',sort {$b cmp $a} @array)

9-8-7-6-5-4-3-2-1-0

join('-',sort {$a cmp $b} @array)

0-1-2-3-4-5-6-7-8-9

join('-',sort lex @array)

 -.-a-a-g-h-k-l-m-n-o-s-t-u-u
```

STACK

Stack is a special data structure used to store data, especially quite useful in function calls. Perl allows to implement stack operation with its inbuilt features. The operation on stack are **push** (insert an element on top of stack), **pop** (remove an element from top of stack), **unshift** (insert an element at the bottom of the stack), **shift** (remove an element from the bottom of the stack). There are four possible combination of stack formed from the above operation.

1. FIFO (First in First Out) – (push/pop)
2. LIFO (Last in First Out) – (unshift/pop)
3. FILO (First in Last Out) – (push/shift)
4. LILO (Last in Last Out) – (unshift/shift)

push @ARRAY, LIST

pop @ARRAY

unshift @ARRAY, LIST

shift @ARRAY

Note that the LIST can be a single element or an array.

Script

```
@array=(0..9);
print "The array contains\n";
print join(',',@array);

print "\n\nPop operation\n";
print "pop \@array=",pop @array;
print "\n\nThe array contains\n";
print join(',',@array);

print "\n\nShift operation\n";
print "shift \@array=",shift @array;
print "\n\nThe array contains\n";
print join(',',@array);

print "\n\nPush operation\n";
print "push \@array, 9=",push @array,9;
print "\n\nThe array contains\n";
print join(',',@array);

print "\n\nUnshift operation\n";
print "unshift \@array,0=",unshift @array,0;
print "\n\nThe array contains\n";
```

```
print join(',',@array);
```

Output

```
G:\Programs\Perl>perl p96.pl
The array contains
0,1,2,3,4,5,6,7,8,9

Pop operation
pop @array=9

The array contains
0,1,2,3,4,5,6,7,8

Shift operation
shift @array=0

The array contains
1,2,3,4,5,6,7,8

Push operation
push @array, 9=9

The array contains
```

```
1,2,3,4,5,6,7,8,9

Unshift operation
unshift @array,0=10

The array contains
0,1,2,3,4,5,6,7,8,9
```

REGULAR EXPRESSIONS

A regular expression is a sequence of string which are used to verify the pattern of a test string. Regular Expression provide an easily way to validate the pattern of the string, instead of using complex function to check it. Even though it performs easy validation it's harder to write. The regular expression binding operator is ~= and !~. The first one is test and assign operator which returns true if string on left follows the pattern specified by the regular expression. The second one is exact reverse that is it return true if the string does not match with pattern specified in the regular expression.

Perl allows three modes of operation, m// called match, s/// called as substitute and tr/// called transliterate. The regular expression is written in-between first // (forward slash) and second. Let us discuss each operator in detail.

Match operator:

The match operator as the name specified matches the string on the left with pattern specified in the right. If it's accepted then a true value is returned. The syntax of match operator is,

m/PATTERN/MODIFIER;

Some of its modifiers are,

i – Ignores case

m – Specify string has a newline or carriage return

o – Evaluate once

s – Use . to match newline

x – Allows whitespace in regular expression

Script

```
#Regular Expression

$txt="Hello how are you? I am fine. I am testing the working of Regular Expression";

print $txt =~/you/;
```

Output

```
G:\Programs\Perl>perl p104.pl

1
```

A value of 1 indicates that the string contains the specified pattern.

Script

```
$str="On One thousand tons online oNto ox ok";

@ons = $str=~ /on/gi;

print join('-',@ons);
```

Output

```
G:\Programs\Perl>perl p105.pl

On-On-on-on-oN
```

The above script finds the words in string starting with ‘on’ globally and ignores cases too. Also it’s stored in an array ‘ons’. Note that instead of m// I have used only //

Match once: The ?PATTERN? is used to match the pattern only once. This is useful when there is a situation where the expression is to be evaluated only once.

Script

```
@list = qw/On One thousand tons online oNto ox ok/;

print "The list contains\n",join('-',@list);

foreach (@list)

{

	$first = $1 if ?(on.*)?i;

	$last = $1 if /(on.*)/i;

	print "\nFirst: $first\nLast: $last";

}

print "\n\nFirst: $first\nLast: $last";
```

Output

```
G:\Programs\Perl>perl p106.pl

Use of ?PATTERN? without explicit operator is deprecated at p106.pl line 7.

The list contains

On-One-thousand-tons-online-oNto-ox-ok
```

```
First: On
Last: On
First: On
Last: One
First: On
Last: One
First: On
Last: ons
First: On
Last: online
First: On
Last: oNto
First: On
Last: oNto
First: On
Last: oNto

First: On
Last: oNto
```

The warning is due to that the operation is deprecated (obsolete) and a newer version is available.

Substitution operator:

The substitution operator is used to replace a pattern by another replacement pattern. This is type of expressions are more useful when the context subject has to be changed to another subject. This operation is similar to Find & Replace in a text document in editors such as Ms Word. The syntax is,

s/PATTERN/REPLACING_PATTERN/MODIFIER;

Substitution operator also allows different quoting styles.

Script

```
$str='The Cat is the cutest animal in the world. I love cats very much. My cat name is Zanny. It loves to play with ball.';

print "The string is \n",$str;

$str =~ s/cat|Cat/hamster/g;

$str =~ s/cats/hamsters/gi;

print "\n\nThe modified string is \n",$str;
```

Output

```
G:\Programs\Perl>perl p107.pl

The string is

The Cat is the cutest animal in the world. I love cats very much. My cat name is Zanny. It loves to play with ball.


The modified string is
```

```
The hamster is the cutest animal in the world.
I love hamsters very much. My hamster name is
Zanny. It loves to play with ball.
```

Delimiters: Substitution allow some delimiters to be used to fetch values from the string that is used. The values can be accessed by variables $1, $2 and so on. The variable $0 holds the name of the file.

\d – Matches a number or a digit

\D – Matches a non-digit or non-number character

\e – Matches an escape sequence

\s – Matches any whitespace character

\S – Matches any non-whitespace character

\z – Matches end of the string

\Z – Matches before end of a newline character

Script

```
$str='04/December/2014';

print $str;

$str=~s|(\d+)/(\S+)/(\d+)|$2 $1, $3|;

print "\n",$str;

$str='04-12-2014';

print "\n\n",$str;

$str=~s{(\d+)-(\d+)-(\d+)}{$2-$1-$3};

print "\n",$str;
```

Output

```
G:\Programs\Perl>perl p108.pl
04/December/2014
December 04, 2014


04-12-2014
12-04-2014
```

Some of the meta-characters used in regular expression are

\ - Treats the next character as a real character not as an operation defined by regular expression. For example, \. Specifies (dot) not as an operation

^ - Matches from start of the string

$ - Matches from end of the string

. – Ignores whitespaces but matches all other characters

| - Specifies another alternate match for same expression

() – Combines operation together as a single unit

[] – Specifies a character class that is a set of characters, for example; [a-z] specifies all lower case alphabets.

* - Indicates zero or more occurrence

+ - Indicates one or more occurrence

Translation or Transliteration operator:

The operation of translation is as similar to substitution operation, but it does not use any regular expression to perform this process. The syntax is,

tr/FIND/REPLACEBY/MODIFIER;

The modifiers are,

c – It complements the FIND list

d – Deletes the un-replaced characters that are found in translation

s – Squash the replaced characters only if it's repeated

Script

```
$str="i typed the string in lower case";

print $str,"\n";

$str=~tr/a-z/A-Z/;

print $str;
```

Output

```
G:\Programs\Perl>perl p112.pl

i typed the string in lower case

I TYPED THE STRING IN LOWER CASE
```

The above is simple transliteration operation to change the case of the string.

Script

```
$str="The cat sat on the mat";

print $str;

$str=~tr/A-Za-z/-/c;

print "\n",$str;
```

Output

```
G:\Programs\Perl>perl p113.pl

The cat sat on the mat

The-cat-sat-on-the-mat
```

The above operation is to replace all non-alpha characters to '-'. In the translation I have specified to replace all alphabets to '-', but in the modifier I have added complement (c), so it replaces only those that are not alphabets.

Script

```
$str="its fun or bun working with perl";

print $str,"\n";

$str=~tr/f-z/*/d;

print $str,"\n";

$str="The food in this restaurant is too good";

print $str,"\n";

$str=~tr/a-z/a-z/s;

print $str;
```

Output

```
G:\Programs\Perl>perl p114.pl

its fun or bun working with perl

 *  b   e

The food in this restaraunt is too good

The fod in this restaraunt is to god
```

The total number of replacements can be counted by assigning to a variable again. The following script demonstrates it.

Script

```
$str="This a string";

print "The string is \"$str\"";

$count=$str=~ tr/a-z|A-Z|0-9| //s;

print "\nThe total number of characters is $count";

print "\nUsing function, total number of characters ",length $str;
```

Output

```
G:\Programs\Perl>perl p115.pl

The string is "This a string"

The total number of characters is 13

Using function, total number of characters 13
```

The above script simply count the number of characters in the string. We can extend it by writing a transliteration to count number of digits only, which is not possible by any inbuilt function.

Regular Expression variables: The following script show the use of $` $& and S' variables.

Script

```
$str="The cat sat on the mat";

$str=~/the/;

print "Before: $`\n";

print "Matched: $&\n";

print "After: $'\n";
```

Output

```
G:\Programs\Perl>perl p120.pl

Before: The cat sat on

Matched: the

After:  mat
```

Elements of Regular Expression: Regular Expression elements are quite useful when you are about match special characters or some entities in a provide string of data. Thus required data can be fetched from string and others can be ignore. Remember while discussing Delimiters in this chapter we used \S, \d. Such can be used for matching operation also which is explained in following script. Note interpolation is also allowed in regular expression.

Script

```
$str="The time is: 12:31:02 on 04/12/2014";

print $str;

$str=~/:\s+/g;

($time)=$str=~/\G(\d+:\d+:\d+)/;

$str=~/.+\s+/g;

($date)=$str=~m{\G(\d+/\d+/\d+)};

print "\n\nTIME: $time\t DATE: $date";
```

Output

```
G:\Programs\Perl>perl p119.pl

The time is: 12:31:02 on 04/12/2015


TIME: 12:31:02   DATE: 04/12/2015
```

ERROR HANDLING MECHANISM

Error handling in the script is one of the major problem many Programmers face. And it's a good habit to handle all types of errors that can arise in script. Error checking and reporting improves the quality of script and reduces malevolent operations.

Method 1:

We can use simple if...else statement to do the error checking which is simplest of all type.

```
if(errorcheck()==0)

{

      die "\nWoah there is an error\n";

}

else

{

      print "\nProgram executed successfully\n";

}

sub errorcheck

{

      $c= int rand(10);

      if($c%2==0)

      {

            return 1;

      }
```

```
        else
        {
                return 0;
        }
}
```

Method 2:

Already we have seen the working of unless statement. Since it acts in reversed of if statement, it can be useful in condition where under false condition the true statement has to be executed.

```
unless(errorcheck()==0)
{
        die "\nWoah there is an error\n";
}
else
{
        print "\nProgram executed successfully\n";
}
sub errorcheck
{
        $c= int rand(10);
        if($c%2==0)
        {
                return 1;
```

```
        }
        else
        {
                return 0;
        }
}
```

Method 3:

Under simpler scripts using if or unless statements increases the line of code, in such cases we can replace them by conditional operator.

```
(errorcheck()==0)? die "\nWoah there is an error\n":print "\nProgram executed successfully\n";

sub errorcheck

{

        $c= int rand(10);

        if($c%2==0)

        {

                return 1;

        }

        else

        {

                return 0;

        }
```

```
}
```

Method 4:

We can use 'or' operation to do error checking. This type of checking is said to be short circuit logic, since in 'or' if one statement is true then entire statement is treated as true and does not evaluate the other one, unless the first statement is false.

```
(errorcheck()==0) or die "\nWoah there is an error\n";

print "\nProgram executed successfully\n";


sub errorcheck

{

      $c= int rand(10);

      if($c%2==0)

      {

            return 1;

      }

      else

      {

            return 0;

      }

}
```

Method 5:

For most of the operation Perl allows to use an in-built error variable to display the type of error occurred. One such example is $! for File handling.

```
open(FILE,"File/abc.txt") or die "File does not exist: $!\nError code:",0+$!,"\n";

close(FILE);
```

Error Reporting:

Error reporting can be done using some inbuilt function, which reports error as well as terminate the executing script safely. The convectional way of reporting error is using if-print logic and added to this, Perl also avails a technique to use the commented lines to display error. Consider the following sample script.

Script

```
print "Before error raise\n";

# line 2 "Error in parsing"

warn "Unrecoverable Error";

print "After error raise\n";
```

Output

```
G:\Programs\Perl>perl p132a.pl

Before error raise

Unrecoverable Error at Error in parsing line 2.

After error raise
```

Note how the comment line goes. It should follow that syntactic way to report the error in either die or warn statements. The way is **# line <number> "message"**. Then only the error is reported in the below used function. Apart from these techniques the following are the available error reporting function available in Perl.

1) <u>Warn function:</u> This is quite useful when some error message has to be displayed if a certain operation is erroneous. The syntax is **warn "$msg"**.

<u>Script</u>

```
print "Before warn function\n";

warn "Executing warn function\n";

print "After warn function\n";
```

<u>Output</u>

```
G:\Programs\Perl>perl p132.pl

Before warn function

Executing warn function

After warn function
```

2) <u>Die function</u>: Sometimes there may be operations which are mandatory and if it's not executed properly then the whole script has to be terminated. In such cases along with message exit operation has to be called, which is performed by this function of syntax **die "$msg"**.

Script

```
print "Before die function\n";
die "Executing die function\n";
print "After die function\n";
```

Output

```
G:\Programs\Perl>perl p131.pl
Before die function
Executing die function
```

Wait a minute! These function did not say the source of the error, only printing the user specified message. This setback can be solved by using **Carp module**. This new module provide another four function which solves the trace overhead of source of error.

3) **Carp function:** This function is similar to the functionality of the warn function added that it prints also the STDERR message along with it. It's used as **carp "$msg"**.

Script

```
#Carp function to raise error
#similar to warn
package T;
use Carp;
```

```
sub err

{     carp "Executing carp function";     }

package main;

sub err1

{     T::err;     }

print "\nBefore carp function";

err1;

print "\nAfter carp function\n";
```

Output

```
G:\Programs\Perl>perl p134.pl


Executing carp function at p134.pl line 9.

Before carp function

After carp function
```

4) Croak function: This function has same functionality of die function and adds an extra feature of reporting of one level up. The syntax is **croak "$msg"**.

Script

```
#Croak function to raise error

#similar to die except it returns report to caller one level up

package T;

use Carp;
```

```
sub err
{     croak "Executing croak function";    }
package main;
sub err1
{     T::err;     }
print "\nBefore croak function";
err1;
print "\nAfter croak function\n";
```

Output

```
G:\Programs\Perl>perl p135.pl


Executing croak function at p135.pl line 9.
Before croak function
```

5) Confess function: This function is similar to cluck and added it prints the stack trace of the error occurred. The syntax is **confess "$msg"**.

Script

```
#Confess function to raise error
#similar to die but it print the stack trace up to original script
package T;
use Carp;
```

```
sub err
{
        confess "Executing confess function";
}
package main;
sub err1
{
        T::err;
}
print "\nBefore confess function";
err1;
print "\nAfter confess function\n";
```

Output

```
G:\Programs\Perl>perl p136.pl


Executing confess function at p136.pl line 6.
        T::err() called at p136.pl line 9
        main::err1() called at p136.pl line 11
Before confess function
```

6) **Cluck function:** This is similar to croak but with an added feature of printing the stack trace. The syntax is **cluck "$msg"**.

Script

```
#Cluck function to raise error

#super charged cluck but it print the stack trace up to original script

package T;

use Carp "cluck";

sub err

{     cluck "Executing cluck function";   }

package main;

sub err1

{     T::err;     }

print "\nBefore cluck function";

err1;

print "\nAfter cluck function\n";
```

Output

```
G:\Programs\Perl>perl p137.pl


Executing cluck function at p137.pl line 6.

        T::err() called at p137.pl line 9

        main::err1() called at p137.pl line 11

Before cluck function

After cluck function
```

This page is intentionally left blank

FILE HANDLING MECHANISM

Giving input manually is highly impossible and tedious in a real time environment, also displaying the output in console for temporary purpose is also inadequate and poor utilization of the resource. In such cases files serves a vital role in perceiving the input and displaying the output. Every programming provides accessing the file system in its own specialized way. In C, file handling is more complicated, that to mainly while reading and writing its byte addressed. Unlike that Perl allows easy way to read into and out of buffers. Also it treats devices are files also.

Most of the function are Unix C like name which are comfortable for the user to remember the function name. The file structure is hold in a variable called as **file handle** which are physical representation of file. These variables are of Type glob nature which is another type of variable in Perl. The STDIN (Write-Only), STDOUT (Read-Only), STDERR (Write-Only) are default file handle provided for any file system. Let us discuss some basic functions performed on files.

1) Opening and Closing Files: Opening a file can be done for many actions such are reading, writing, appending and combined actions. The arguments take native form of shell scripting to specify the action. The syntax is **open FILEHANDLE, EXPR**. And for closing the file **close FILEHANDLE** is used. The close function is not mandatory as file is automatically closed once the script terminates. But it's always a good practice to close an opened file unless it's needed for future in same mode as it's opened before.

For open function the arguments in EXPR are: > to write into a file, < to read from file, + to append to the file at the current position of file pointer without truncating, >> to append at the end of file (no read), +>> to append at end and also read.

Another way of opening file is to use the **sysopen** function which avoid the confusion in EXPR in open function. The syntax is **sysopen FILEHANDLE, FILE_NAME, OPEN_MODE**. The OPEN_MODE contains bits that performs specified operation. The bit set can be done using predefine variables defined in module **IO::File**. Some of the bit set modes are O_CREAT, O_RDONLY, OWRONLY, O_RDWR, O_TRUNC ..., etc.

2) Reading from and Writing to Files: Now that the FILEHANDLE is pointed to the file now actions such as reading and writing can be performed on them. Perl offers easy reading process through file handles. The way to read from a file using file handle is **$var=<FILEHANDLE>**. Also another way is to use functions such as **readline DATA** or **read FILEHANDLE, DATA, DATA_LENGTH [, OFFSET]**. Similarly the **sysread FILEHANDLE, DATA, LENGTH [,OFFSET]** can also be used, the difference is that **sysread** allows unbuffered operation.

Now in same context we can perform write operation by simply replacing read by write. That is **write FILEHANDLE, BUFFER, BUFFER_LENGTH [, OFFSET]** or **syswrite FILEHANDLE, BUFFER, BUFFER_LENGTH [, OFFSET]** which allows unbuffered operation. Even the print function in the form **print FILEHANDLE, DATA** can be used to write data.

3) Current position of File pointer: To find the current position of the file pointer the **tell FILEHANDLE** can be used, which returns an integer value of the position of the file pointer. It returns **undef** if there is problem in file.

4) Move File pointer to specified position: To move across the file the function **seek FILEHANDLE, POSITION, FROM_WHERE** where POSITION specifies number of bytes to be traversed, FROM_WHERE specifies from which place POSITION has to be adjusted, which can be start (**SEEK_SET**), current position (**SEEK_CUR**) or end (**SEEK_END**). These constants are available in **IO::Seekable**.

5) Binary mode of File: To change the mode from text to binary for file the function **binmode FILEHANLDE** can be used. Once you set the binary mode on there is no way to unset it back rather closing it and reopening it again.

6) End of File: To check whether the next byte to read is the end of file character, the function **eof FILEHANDLE** can be used. It returns true when it reaches the end of file.

7) File Number: The file number of the file in the file descriptor table is returned through the function **fileno FILEHANDLE**. This is more helpful while handling multiple files in such cases there maybe two different file handles referencing same file, which is more dangerous. In these times we can use file number (which is unique) to compare whether any two file handles refers a same file.

8) <u>**Truncate a File:**</u> To empty the content of file either fully or of specified length the function **truncate FILEHANDLE [, LENGTH]** can be used.

9) <u>**File Information and Details:**</u> Every operating system maintains a data structure called inode to store the details about the file. We can get the information using **stat $FILENAME**. It returns a list in following order:

(Device_No, Inode_No, File_Mode, No_Of_Links, User_ID, Group_ID, Device_ID, Size, Last_Access_Time, Last_Modified_Time, Inode_Change_Time, Block_Size, Allocated_Blocks) = stat $FILENAME;

Note the File_Mode values is returned as octal value which later handled by programmer for his convenience to display as UNIX like view.

10) <u>**Rename the File:**</u> The purpose of renaming is to avoid clash of file names especially while moving files across directories. The syntax is **rename $oldfilename, $newfilename**

11) <u>**Accessing Directories:**</u> Similar to files directories also requires access to create/remove a file or change from one directory to another. The following are allowed operations:

opendir DIRHANDLE, EXPR

closedir DIRHANDLE

telldir DIRHANDLE

seekdir DIRHANDLE, POSITION

chdir $DIRECTORY

12) Get Current Working Directory: The current working directory can be known by using the function **getcwd** available in the **Cwd** module.

13) Locking Files: The file locks are provided so that in a multiprocessing environment, we can avoid several process accessing it simultaneously. It can be performed using **flock FILEHANDLE, LOCK**. The LOCK can be **LOCK_SH** (Shared Lock), **LOCK_EX** (Exclusive Lock), **LOCK_UN** (Unlock), **LOCK_NB** (Lock without any blocks).

Script

```
#File handling

open(DATA,"<    Files/sample.txt")    ||    die
$!,"\nFile not found\n";

@lines=<DATA>;

print @lines;

close DATA;
```

sample.txt

```
An apple a day keeps the doctor away.

Banana is rich in potassium.

Orange is good for your eyes.

Figs are rich in Iron content.

Chipko are good for blood.
```

Output

```
G:\Programs\Perl\FileHandling>perl pf1.pl
```

```
An apple a day keeps the doctor away.

Banana is rich in potassium.

Orange is good for your eyes.

Figs are rich in Iron content.

Chipko are good for blood.
```

Script

```
my $file="Files/sample.txt";

my
($mode,$nlinks,$uid,$gid,$size,$mtime)=(stat($f
ile))[2..5,7,9];

printf("%s %2d %8d %s
%s\n",$mode,$nlinks,$size,scalar
localtime($mtime),$file);
```

Output

```
G:\Programs\Perl\FileHandling>perl pf2.pl

33206  1       158  Fri  Dec  19  22:17:48  2014
Files/sample.txt
```

Script

```
use Cwd;

print getcwd(),"\n";
```

Output

```
G:\Programs\Perl\FileHandling>perl pf3.pl
```

G:/Programs/Perl/FileHandling

Script

```
#Handling directory

opendir(DIR,'G:/ Programs/Perl/FileHandling') or
die "Cant open the directory\n",$!,"\n";

while($f =readdir DIR)

{ print "$f\t"; }

use Cwd;

chdir('G:/ Programs/Perl/FileHandling/Files') or
die "\nCant change directory\n",$!,"\n";

print "\nCurrent working directory
",getcwd(),"\n";

opendir(DIR,getcwd()) or die "Cant open the
directory\n",$!,"\n";

while($f =readdir DIR)

{ print "$f\t"; }

closedir DIR or die "\nCant close the
directory\n",$!,"\n";
```

Output

```
G:\Programs\Perl\FileHandling>perl pf4.pl

.        ..        FileHandler.pm  Files   pf1.pl
pf2.pl  pf2a.pl pf3.pl  pf4.pl  pf5.pl  pf6.pl

Current                  working                directory
G:/Programs/Perl/FileHandling/Files

.          ..          samp.txt            samp1.txt
sample.txt       sample2.txt
```

Script

```
use IO::File;

sysopen(FP,"Files/sample2.txt",O_CREAT |
O_WRONLY) or die "\nCant create the file or
",$!,"\n";

print "Enter some text\n";

$text=<STDIN>; chomp $text;

syswrite(FP,"$text\n",length $text); close FP;

sysopen(FP,"Files/sample2.txt",O_RDONLY) or die
"\nCant open the file or ",$!,"\n";

print $text while((sysread(FP,$text,256)));

close FP;
```

sample2.txt

```
An apple a day keeps the doctor away.Banana is
rich in potassium.Orange is good for your
eyes.Figs are rich in Iron content.Chipko are
good for blood.
```

Output

```
G:\Programs\Perl\FileHandling>perl pf5.pl

Enter some text

An apple a day keeps the doctor away.

An apple a day keeps the doctor away.Banana is
rich in potassium.Orange is good for your
eyes.Figs are rich in Iron content.Chipko are
good for blood.
```

OBJECT ORIENTED PROGRAMING

Object oriented programming is one of the most intriguing feature in any programming languages. It helps to represent real time entity in script and define feature and behaviors to that entity. But sadly Perl doesn't provide object oriented programming feature. Then why a separate chapter? In this we emulate the feature of object oriented programming using Perl's flavors. That is we are going to create a typical OOP script in Perl using its feature, which is with the help of packages. Also note that the object here are mere references created by programmer. To know more let's get clear with three terms: *Object* is a reference to a collection of variables or it's the real time entity of class. *Class* is a template for object, which contains methods and attributes (variables). *Method* is simply subroutines defined in Perl.

Creating Class:

The class in Perl is basically created using packages. The methods are written under it and later used in script.

Creating Objects:

The reader of this book (if familiar if an OOP language) might know that to create an object we need a **constructor**, which initializes the object. The constructor is written by the programmer. But an additional overhead is that now programmer has to initialize the object by writing inside the constructor. Conventionally **new** is the method which is use to initialize object or call the constructor. The initialization can be done through *blessing* of an object.

Destroying Objects:

Most programming language such as Java has inbuilt garbage collectors to handle unused and out of scope objects. In Perl since we emulate the concept we must define our own destruction mechanism in the subroutine called **DESTROY**. Perl calls this method upon freeing the space for the object. Note Perl only destroys the object reference and not the internal data structures referred by the object.

Creation Syntax:

Class is created as below:

```
package ClassName;
sub new
{
        my $object=shift;
        my $var={};
        bless $var, $object;
        return $object;
}
sub otherMethods
{
        #Body of the subroutine
}
sub DESTROY
{
```

```
        #Body of DESTROY
}
```

Now to create an object:

```
use ClassName;
$obj= new ClassName(intial_arguments);
```

The method is called as:

```
$obj->otherMethods();
```

The entire class creation is written in a .pm file and the additional statements such as exporting the module are also included in them.

Let us see an example of the entire concept:

Script

Sample.pm

```
package Sample; #Class
require Exporter;
@ISA=(Exporter);
@Export=(new,getname,getroll);
sub new                     #constructor
{
      my $obj=shift;
      my $var={
                        'Name'=>shift,
                        'Rollno'=>shift
```

```
                };
        bless $var,$obj;
        return $var;
}

sub getname
{
        my ($var)=@_;
        return $var->{'Name'};
}

sub getroll
{
        my ($var)=@_;
        return $var->{'Rollno'};
}
1;
```

po1.pl

```
use Sample;
$obj=new Sample("Gokul",305);
print $obj;
print "\nName:",$obj->getname();
print "\nRollno:",$obj->getroll();
```

Output

```
G:\Programs\Perl\OOP>perl po1.pl
Sample=HASH(0xe8d208)
Name:Gokul
Rollno:305
```

Inheritance:

The most useful concept of OOP is *inheritance* which is nothing but deriving property of one class called base class to another class called derived class. Thus it gives more powerful way to reuse the predefined features.

One such example is discussed below: Here the base class is Animal and has sub classes Tiger and Wolf. The both class in turn derived in single level as Dog and Cat. The partially constructed class diagram is:

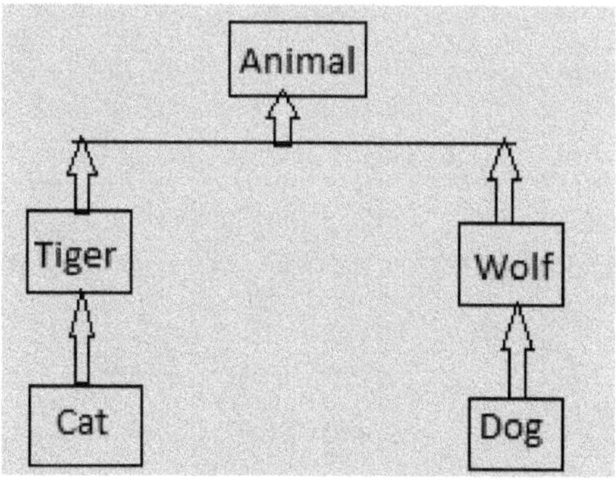

The features of Animal is available in Tiger as well as in cat. Also the feature of tiger is available in Cat. Same way the other branch goes. The coding for each class is done in separate .pm file to increase the reusability. Thus various type of inheritance models can be constructed by simply defining packages. How we import the feature is by requiring the package in the required place.

Script

Animal.pm

```
package Animal;
require Exporter;
@ISA=(Exporter);
sub new
{
      my $obj=shift;
      my $var={};
      bless $var,$obj;
      return $var;
}
sub move
{
      my $a=shift;
      $a=~ /=/;
      print "\n$` is moving";
}
sub sleep
{
```

```
      my $a=shift;
      $a=~ /=/;
      print "\n$` is sleeping";
}
```

Tiger.pm

```
package Tiger;
require Animal;
our @ISA=(Animal);
sub new
{
      my $obj=shift;
      my $var={};
      bless $var,$obj;
      return $var;
}
sub roar
{
      my $a=shift;
      $a=~ /=/;
      print "\n$` is roaring";
}
```

Wolf.pm

```
package Wolf;
require Animal;
our @ISA=(Animal);
sub new
{
	my $obj=shift;
	my $var={};
	bless $var,$obj;
	return $var;
}
sub howl
{
	my $a=shift;
	$a=~ /=/;
	print "\n$` is howling";
}
```

Cat.pm

```
package Cat;
require Tiger;
our @ISA=(Tiger);
sub new
{
```

```
	my $obj=shift;
	my $var={};
	bless $var,$obj;
	return $var;
}
sub mew
{
	my $a=shift;
	$a=~ /=/;
	print "\n$` is mewing";
}
```

Dog.pm

```
package Dog;
require Wolf;
our @ISA=(Wolf);
sub new
{
	my $obj=shift;
	my $var={};
	bless $var,$obj;
	return $var;
}
sub bark
```

```
{
      my $a=shift;
      $a=~ /=/;
      print "\n$` is barking";
}
```

po2.pl

```
use Animal;
$animal=new Animal();
print $animal;
$animal->move();
$animal->sleep();
no Animal;

print "\n\n";
use Tiger;
$tiger=new Tiger();
print $tiger;
$tiger->move();
$tiger->sleep();
$tiger->roar();
no Tiger;

print "\n\n";
```

```
use Wolf;
$wolf=new Wolf();
print $wolf;
$wolf->move();
$wolf->sleep();
$wolf->howl();
no Wolf;

print "\n\n";
use Cat;
$cat=new Cat();
print $cat;
$cat->move();
$cat->sleep();
$cat->mew();
$cat->roar();
no Cat;

print "\n\n";
use Dog;
$dog=new Dog();
print $dog;
$dog->move();
```

```
$dog->sleep();
$dog->bark();
$dog->howl();
no Dog;
```

Output

```
G:\Programs\Perl\OOP>perl po2.pl
Animal=HASH(0x1dd208)
Animal is moving
Animal is sleeping

Tiger=HASH(0x1dd310)
Tiger is moving
Tiger is sleeping
Tiger is roaring

Wolf=HASH(0x1dd3d0)
Wolf is moving
Wolf is sleeping
Wolf is howling

Cat=HASH(0x22d4e90)
Cat is moving
Cat is sleeping
```

```
Cat is mewing
Cat is roaring

Dog=HASH(0x22d4fb0)
Dog is moving
Dog is sleeping
Dog is barking
Dog is howling
```

The statement **no MODULENAME** can be used to un-import the imported package.

AUTOLOAD method:

There may be some cases where the user call to an undefined method which results in unnecessary error or some simple execution does not need a method call, in such cases we define AUTOLOAD subroutine to load on encountering unfound method.

Script

Parents.pm

```
package Parents;
require Exporter;
@ISA=(Exporter);
```

```
sub new
{
      print "\nParent is created";
      my $obj=shift;
      my $var={};
      bless $var,$obj;
      return $var;
}
sub pmethod
{
      print "\nParent method is called";
}
sub AUTOLOAD
{
      my $a=$AUTOLOAD;
      $a=~ s/.*:://;
      print "\n$a method is not found";
}
sub DESTROY
{
      print "\nParent is destroyed";
}
1;
```

Child.pm

```
package Child;
require Parents;
our @ISA=(Parents);
sub new
{
      print "\nChild is created";
      my $obj=shift;
      my $var={};
      bless $var,$obj;
      return $var;
}
sub cmethod
{
      print "\nChild method is called";
}
sub DESTROY
{
      print "\nChild is destroyed";
}
```

po3.pl

```
use Parents;
use Child;
```

```
$parent = new Parents();
$parent->pmethod();
$parent->unknown();
print "\n\n";
$chd=new Child();
$chd->pmethod();
$chd->cmethod();
$chd->unknown();
print "\n\n";
```

Real Time Example:

Consider the file handling scenario to read and write data on a file.

Script

FileHandler.pm

```
package FileHandler;
require Exporter;
@ISA=(Exporter);
use IO::File;
sub new
{
	$obj=shift;
	$var={'Fname'=>shift};
```

```
        sysopen(F,"$var->{'Fname'}",O_CREAT,0666)
|| die "Unable to create the file: $!\nError
code: ",0+$!,"\n";

        close F;

        bless $var,$obj;

        return $var;

}

sub readFromFile

{

        open(F,$var->{'Fname'}) || die "Unable to
open the file: $!\nError code: ",0+$!,"\n";

        my @list=<F>;

        print @list;

        close F;

}

sub writeToFile

{

        sysopen(F,$var->{'Fname'},O_WRONLY) ||
die "Unable to open the file: $!\nError code:
",0+$!,"\n";

        shift;

        my $a;

        syswrite(F,$a,length $a) while($a=shift);

        close F;

}
```

pf6.pl

```
use FileHandler;
$f= new FileHandler("Files/samp.txt");
$file="Files/sample.txt";
open(F,$file) || die "Error cant open: $!\n";
@lines=<F>;
close F;
$f->writeToFile(@lines);
$f->readFromFile();
```

<u>Output</u>

```
G:\Programs\Perl\FileHandling>perl pf6.pl
An apple a day keeps the doctor away.
Banana is rich in potassium.
Orange is good for your eyes.
Figs are rich in Iron content.
Chipko are good for blood.
```

REFERENCES (POINTERS)

References or simply Pointers are variables which points to another variable. These points to a data or another reference. We classify them into two types: *Symbolic (Soft)* and *Hard* reference. Compared to C, I would say Perl have more elegance in accessing these references.

Symbolic (Soft) Reference is a facility to address a variable by its name which is a data content of another variable. Confused?? We will see this concept with an example pretty soon in the later part of the chapter. *Hard Reference* is like pointer we conventionally use in C, which is using the address of a variable to access the data of the variable. It simply a variable which holds the address of the data to be accessed. From the above concept we have two process namely *referencing,* which is encoding the data in some structured way and *dereferencing,* which is extracting the information from those created structure.

Script

```
#Creating symbolic (soft) reference

$name="Gokul";

$attr="name";

print "Soft References\n";

print "\$name=$name has symbolic reference
\$\$attr=$$attr\n\n";
```

```
#Creating hard reference
sub function
{
	1;
}
$var="Hello";
@arr=(1..5);
%hash=('a'=>1,'b'=>2);
$refv=\$var;
$refa=\@arr;
$refh=\%hash;
$refsr=\&function;
$refglob=\*STDOUT;
print "Hard References\n";
print "\$var=$var has reference $refv\n";
print "\@arr=@arr has reference $refa\n";
print "\%hash=",%hash," has reference $refh\n";
print "sub function=",function," has reference
$refsr\n";
print "STDOUT has reference $refglob\n";
```

Output

```
G:\Programs\Perl>perl p138.pl
Soft References
```

```
$name=Gokul has symbolic reference $$attr=Gokul


Hard References
$var=Hello has reference SCALAR(0x2340a70)
@arr=1 2 3 4 5 has reference ARRAY(0x2340ab8)
%hash=b2a1 has reference HASH(0x2340c50)
sub function=1 has reference CODE(0x23409e0)
STDOUT has reference GLOB(0x23400f8)
```

The above script demonstrates the referencing concept. See that how the soft reference are created. The internal process done here is, in '$$attr' for '$attr' it's replaced by the value 'name', so now Perl evaluates as '$name' which is nothing but 'Gokul'. For creating the hard reference \ is used in front of all types. What here goes is that the address of the particular type is fetched from the symbol table along with its data type and stored in the respective variable.

With these reference concept we have newer concepts such as Anonymous array, hashes and subroutines & data structure of data structure such as Array of array ..., etc.

Anonymous Array, Hashes and Subroutine:

Here the array is specified and accessed without any name to it, hence the name anonymous. These have only address or reference to access them. Consider the below script, where an array contain another array which is directly specified inside another without any name. These type of concepts are helpful when the data are accessed only once or twice in a particular block alone.

Script

```
#Anonymous array
$ar=[1,2,3,4,5];
print $ar,"\n";
@aoa=(1,2,[3,4,5,6,[7,8,9,10]]);
print join("\t",@aoa),"\n";
$aoar=[1,2,[3,4,5,6,[7,8,9,10]]];
print $aoar,"\n";
```

Output

```
G:\Programs\Perl>perl p140.pl
ARRAY(0xd0d208)
1       2       ARRAY(0x22b4fc8)
ARRAY(0x22c0da0)
```

Similar to arrays we can do anonymous hashing to the data, which is explained in following script.

Script

```
#Anonymous hashes
$hash={'a'=>1,'b'=>2};
print $hash,"\n";
```

Output

```
G:\Programs\Perl>perl p141.pl
HASH(0x1fd208)
```

In the same way we have anonymous subroutines which are accessible through their address. The following script demonstrate it.

Script

```
#Anonymous subroutines
$sr=sub { print "\nHello\n"; };
print $sr;
```

Output

```
G:\Programs\Perl>perl p142.pl
CODE(0x2310890)
```

In the above script see after sub no name is specified here, hence the subroutine becomes anonymous.

Dereferencing:

The dereferencing operation is used to get the data from these complex structures. The dereferencing for each structure is discussed below.

1) Array:

To dereference the array we have to use double dollar sign, that is **$$arrayname[index]** is used. See the following script to understand the dereference operation.

Script

```
#Dereferencing the array
@arr=(1..5);
$rfa=\@arr;
print "\$rfa=$rfa\n";
print "\@arr=@arr\n";
$_=0;
do
{
        print "\n\$\$rfa[$_]=$$rfa[$_]";
        $_++;
}while($$rfa[$_]);
```

2) Hashes:

The dereferencing of the hashes is done by **$$hashname{'key'}**. See the following example

Script

```
#Dereferencing hashes
$hash={'a'=>1,'b'=>2};
print "\$hash=$hash\n";
```

```
print "\$\$hash{'a'}=$$hash{'a'}\n";
```

3) Subroutines:

The dereferencing can be done in two ways either, **&$subr** or **$subr->()**, which is explained in below script.

Script

```
#Dereferencing the subroutines

$rsb=sub { print "This is the sub routine\n";
};

sub func

{

      print "This is func subroutine\n";

}

$rsb1=\&func;

print "\$rsb=$rsb\n";

print "\$rsb1=$rsb1\n";

&$rsb;

$rsb->();

&$rsb1;
```

4) Globs:

The globs are normally accessed using **<$gl>** in script and directly as **$gl** if specified as parameter.

Script

```
#Dereferencing Globs
```

```
$rgb=\*STDOUT;
print $rgb "Perl is cool!\n";
print "Enter a value\t";
$rgb1=\*STDIN;
$a=<$rgb1>;
print "\nYou entererd $a";
```

5) Array of array:

The array of array can be dereferenced using **->** operator. The number of -> depends on number of dereferencing operation. For example, if there array which in turn contains another array, then to access the element in second array it's done as **$$arr[index m]->[index n]**.

Script

```
#Dereferencing array of array
$aoa=[1,2,[3,4,[5,6]]];
print "\$aoa=$aoa\n";
print "\$\$aoa[0]=$$aoa[0]\n";
print "\$\$aoa[1]=$$aoa[1]\n";
print "\$\$aoa[2]=$$aoa[2]\n";
print "\$\$aoa[2]->[0]=$$aoa[2]->[0]\n";
print "\$\$aoa[2]->[1]=$$aoa[2]->[1]\n";
print "\$\$aoa[2]->[2]=$$aoa[2]->[2]\n";
print      "\$\$aoa[2]->[2]->[0]=$$aoa[2]->[2]-
>[0]\n";
```

```
print       "\$\$aoa[2]->[2]->[1]=$$aoa[2]->[2]-
>[1]\n";
```

Output

```
G:\Programs\Perl>perl p148.pl

$aoa=ARRAY(0xc34f20)

$$aoa[0]=1

$$aoa[1]=2

$$aoa[2]=ARRAY(0xd2d3d0)

$$aoa[2]->[0]=3

$$aoa[2]->[1]=4

$$aoa[2]->[2]=ARRAY(0xd2d208)

$$aoa[2]->[2]->[0]=5

$$aoa[2]->[2]->[1]=6
```

6) Hashes of Hashes:

The same way as in array of array, the dereferencing of a two level hash, in which the element of second hash to be accessed, we use **$hash{'key1'}->{'key2'}.**

Script

```
#Dereferencing hashes of hashes;

$hash={'fruit'=>{'apple'=>10,'banana'=>5,'orang
e'=>8},'vegetable'=>{'onion'=>12,'ladysfinger'=
>4,'potato'=>7},'grain'=>{'moong'=>6,'oor'=>4,'
wheat'=>5}};

print "\$hash=$hash\n";
```

```
print "\$hash->{'fruit'}=$hash->{'fruit'}\n";

print "\$hash->{'vegetable'}=$hash-
>{'vegetable'}\n";

print "\$hash->{'grain'}=$hash->{'grain'}\n";

print "\$hash->{'fruit'}->{'apple'}=$hash-
>{'fruit'}->{'apple'}\n";

print "\$hash->{'vegetable'}-
>{'ladysfinger'}=$hash->{'vegetable'}-
>{'ladysfinger'}\n";

print "\$hash->{'grain'}->{'wheat'}=$hash-
>{'grain'}->{'wheat'}\n";
```

Output

```
G:\Programs\Perl>perl p149.pl

$hash=HASH(0x690e30)

$hash->{'fruit'}=HASH(0xe3d208)

$hash->{'vegetable'}=HASH(0x684e48)

$hash->{'grain'}=HASH(0x684f38)

$hash->{'fruit'}->{'apple'}=10

$hash->{'vegetable'}->{'ladysfinger'}=4

$hash->{'grain'}->{'wheat'}=5
```

7) Array of Hashes:

For this concept let us assume an array which contain number of hashes, then to access the data in hashes **$arrofhash[index]{‘key’}**.

Script

```
#Arrays of Hashes

@aoh=({'a'=>{1=>'apple',2=>'apricot'},'b'=>{1=>
'banana',2=>'bellpepper'}},{'A'=>{1=>'Aeroplane
',2=>'Ant'},'B'=>{1=>'Ball',2=>'Banjo'}});

print "\@aoh=@aoh\n";

print "\$aoh[0]=$aoh[0]\n";

print "\$aoh[1]=$aoh[1]\n";

print "\$aoh[0]{'a'}=$aoh[0]{'a'}\n";

print "\$aoh[0]{'a'}->{1}=$aoh[0]{'a'}->{1}\n";

print "\$aoh[0]{'a'}{2}=$aoh[0]{'a'}{2}\n";

print "\$aoh[0]{'b'}=$aoh[0]{'b'}\n";

print "\$aoh[0]{'b'}->{1}=$aoh[0]{'b'}->{1}\n";

print "\$aoh[0]{'b'}{2}=$aoh[0]{'b'}{2}\n";

print "\$aoh[1]{'A'}=$aoh[1]{'A'}\n";

print "\$aoh[1]{'A'}->{1}=$aoh[1]{'A'}->{1}\n";

print "\$aoh[1]{'A'}{2}=$aoh[1]{'A'}{2}\n";

print "\$aoh[1]{'B'}=$aoh[1]{'B'}\n";

print "\$aoh[1]{'B'}->{1}=$aoh[1]{'B'}->{1}\n";

print "\$aoh[1]{'B'}{2}=$aoh[1]{'B'}{2}\n";
```

Output

```
G:\Programs\Perl>perl p154.pl

@aoh=HASH(0x2264e78) HASH(0x2284998)
```

```
$aoh[0]=HASH(0x2264e78)
$aoh[1]=HASH(0x2284998)
$aoh[0]{'a'}=HASH(0x1dd208)
$aoh[0]{'a'}->{1}=apple
$aoh[0]{'a'}{2}=apricot
$aoh[0]{'b'}=HASH(0x1dd3d0)
$aoh[0]{'b'}->{1}=banana
$aoh[0]{'b'}{2}=bellpepper
$aoh[1]{'A'}=HASH(0x2264fc8)
$aoh[1]{'A'}->{1}=Aeroplane
$aoh[1]{'A'}{2}=Ant
$aoh[1]{'B'}=HASH(0x2284c80)
$aoh[1]{'B'}->{1}=Ball
$aoh[1]{'B'}{2}=Banjo
```

8) Hashes of Array:

Now consider hashes that contains array as key and array as array of data, then to access the hash whose data is array, **$hashofarr{'key'}[index]**; and if key is array, **$hashofarr{$arrofkey}[index]**.

Script

```
#hashes of arrays
$s=[2,22];
```

```
%hoa=(1=>['a','A'],$s=>['b','B']);
print "\%hoa=",%hoa,"\n";
print "\$hoa{1}=$hoa{1}\n";
print "\$hoa{1}[0]=$hoa{1}[0]\n";
print "\$hoa{1}->[1]=$hoa{1}->[1]\n";
print "\$s=$s\n";
print "\$hoa{\$s}=$hoa{$s}\n";
print "\$hoa{\$s}[0]=$hoa{$s}[0]\n";
print "\$hoa{\$s}->[1]=$hoa{$s}->[1]\n";
```

Output

```
G:\Programs\Perl>perl p155.pl
%hoa=1ARRAY(0xd2d388)ARRAY(0xd2d208)ARRAY(0x22d
4e90)
$hoa{1}=ARRAY(0xd2d388)
$hoa{1}[0]=a
$hoa{1}->[1]=A
$s=ARRAY(0xd2d208)
$hoa{$s}=ARRAY(0x22d4e90)
$hoa{$s}[0]=b
$hoa{$s}->[1]=B
```

Determining the Reference type:

It's mandatory to know what type of reference we are dealing with in a complex script. For this purpose an inbuilt function called **ref** is used.

Script

```
#determining the reference type
$var="hello";
$rvar=\$var;
print "\$var=$var\t\$rvar=$rvar\n";
print "ref \$var=",ref $var;
print "\nref \$rvar=",ref $rvar;
```

Output

```
G:\Programs\Perl>perl p150.pl
$var=hello      $rvar=SCALAR(0x22c07e8)
ref $var=
ref $rvar=SCALAR
```

PROCESS HANDLING

Process are just running program in the system. Such can be an application program or system program. Process is key part of your system to perform specified task. Process can create another process or can also destroy it. In UNIX system, the first process loaded on the memory creates another process called **init** which is the first child process created, does the swapping process in the memory system. So process creation and handling are important task. In Windows system process running in operating system are not transparent entirely. But still we have the ability of see some of the underlying process using Task Manager.

Process requires communication also which help to achieve some important task. This task of communication between the processes is called *interprocess communication.* Further in this chapter we will see how to create, control and manage process.

Creating Process: The process can be created using function called **fork**. This newly created process is called as *child process.*

What fork does is, it creates a copy of entire script after the fork function call into a separate address space. Then simultaneously the parent process and the child process starts to run. The jobs for each process can be assigned using the if...else block. Now how to identify which is child and which is parent? This can be done using the return value of the fork function call.

If the returned value is *non zero* then it's *parent process* and if it's *equal to zero* its *child process*. That is on success of execution these criteria must be satisfied. On *failure of fork, undef* value is returned.

I am keeping on rambling about some value, you must be now curious what that value specifies and it's nothing but *ProcessID*. Each process running in the system is assigned with this unique id. The process id of any process can be obtained through **getppid** function call. But sadly this is available for UNIX system only. So for Windows, we have a secret variable **$$** which will contains the process id of the currently executing process, so Windows users no worries. I am also using Windows only so I use $$ only.

So we define the fork return value clearly as; on successful execution, the parent get the value of child process id and for child 0 (zero) is returned.

Let's see an example how to create a simple process in Perl. See the following script.

<u>Script</u>

```
print "I am parent ID=$$","\n";

$child=fork;

if($child<0)

{     print "I am parent again ID=$$","\n";
      }

else

{     print "I am child ID=$$","\n";       }
```

Output

```
G:\Programs\Perl\Process Handling>perl pp1.pl

I am parent ID=336

I am parent again ID=336

I am child ID=-6736
```

The process id differs for each system and on each execution.

Destroying Process: Eventually as the task of the process completes the process is automatically destroyed from the address space. But there may be several cases where the child may outlive the parent in such cases we can use the function **kill SIGKILL, @pid** to destroy the process. Where SIGKILL is an inbuilt Perl variable with value and @pid contains list of process id's.

Script

```
print "I am parent ID=$$","\n";

$child=fork;

if($child<0)

{

      print "I am parent again ID=$$ with
ID=$child","\n";

      kill SIGKILL,$child;

}

else
```

```
{
      print "I am child ID=$$","\n";
      sleep 5;
}
```

Output

```
G:\Programs\Perl\Process Handling>perl pp2.pl
I am parent ID=7540
I am parent again ID=7540 with ID=-5016
I am child ID=-5016
```

Without sleeping the process immediately terminates. This can only be experienced when you work with Perl. The Sleep function is already discussed in previous chapters, so let's move on to other topics.

Signaling the process: A function call to kill will always terminate the specified process. In order to signal the process alone and perform user defined action we use an environmental variable hash called **%SIG**, in which we specify a pointer to subroutine. The function **kill CONST, @pid**, some of the CONST value are

SIGKILL – To kill the process immediately

SIGALRM – To terminate the process by signaling an alarm

SIGABRT – Abnormal Termination of the process

SIGFPE – Termination due to Arithmetic Exception

SIGILL – Termination due to illegal instruction

SIGINT – Interrupt from any process or device (like keyboard (Ctrl + C))

SIGPIPE – Termination due to illegal write on pipe

SIGQUIT – Quit signal from application or device to kill

SIGSTOP – Stop the specified process using stop signal

SIGCONT – Continue the stopped process

SIGCHLD – Signal of child termination or end

The **alarm $num** can be used, which raises alarm signal to process in 'num' seconds. Note alarm works only in the UNIX system.

See the following code to know the available signals:

Script

```
foreach $signal (sort keys %SIG)

{

      print "$signal,";

}
```

Output

```
G:\Programs\Perl\Process Handling>perl pp3.pl

ABRT,ALRM,BREAK,CHLD,CLD,CONT,FPE,HUP,ILL,INT,K
ILL,NUM05,NUM06,NUM07,NUM10,NUM12,NUM16,NUM17,N
UM18,NUM19,NUM24,PIPE,QUIT,SEGV,STOP,TERM,
```

Script

```
sub sig

{

      my $signal=shift;

      print "Got the signal $signal from
user\n";

      $SIG{$signal}=\&sig;

      exit 1;

}


$SIG{INT} = \&sig;

for(;;){}
```

Output

```
G:\Programs\Perl\Process Handling>perl pp4.pl

Got the signal INT from user
```

The output above is obtained once you press the keys (Ctrl + C) which generates the interrupt. We manually override the default subroutine for the interrupt generation here.

Now we see how to handle signals that are raised from program due to warn and die functions. The user defined warning and die routines can be overridden by __WARN__ and __DIE__ which are used in %SIG as keys. Let's see an example.

Script

```
sub user_die
{
	my ($err)= @_;
	die "Trapped this: $err";
}

sub user_warn
{
	my ($err)= @_;
	warn "Trapped this: $err";
}

$SIG{__WARN__}= \&user_warn;
warn "You are under critical warning!";

$SIG{__DIE__}= \&user_die;
die "Critical Error occurred!";
```

Output

```
G:\Programs\Perl\Process Handling>perl pp5.pl
Trapped this: You are under critical warning!
at pp5.pl line 14.
```

```
Trapped this: Critical Error occurred! at
pp5.pl line 17.
```

Hence during any warn or die operation we can properly handle the unhandled task such as closing a file or terminate all the alive child process properly without leaving them as zombies and so on.

Assigning job to process: This can be done using the **exec** function or using **system** function. The basic difference between these two is that exec directly execute the parameter on current process address space, whereas the system forks a new process and executes it.

exec $PROGRAM,@ARG_FOR_PRGM;

system $PROGRAM,@ARG_FOR_PRGM; or

system "$PROGRAM $ARG1 … $ARGn"

Script

```
if(@ARGV>=1)
{
	print "Argument: ";
	foreach $a (@ARGV)
	{	print "$a ";		}
	print "\n";
}
else
```

```
{     print "No Argument\n";  }
$child=fork;
if($child<0)
{
      print scalar localtime;
      print "\n";
}
else
{
      if(@ARGV==0)
      {
            print "\nChild executing perl
pp5.pl\n";
            exec "perl","pp5.pl";
      }
      elsif(@ARGV>=1)
      {
            print "\nChild executing date/T\n";
            system "date/T";
      }
}
```

Output

```
G:\Programs\Perl\Process Handling>perl pp6.pl
```

```
No Argument

Sun Dec 20 13:31:12 2015


Child executing perl pp5.pl

Trapped this: You are under critical warning! at pp5.pl line 14.

Trapped this: Critical Error occured! at pp5.pl line 17.


G:\Programs\Perl\Process Handling>perl pp6.pl 1

Argument: 1

Sun Dec 20 13:31:15 2015


Child executing date/T

Sun 12/20/2015
```

Orphan Process: Orphan process is a special or abnormal case where *the child process may outlive the parent process.* That is the parent process terminates before the child completes its process. Such process is left abandoned and will may persist in the address space consuming the memory available. But for such situations in UNIX the **init** process adopts the child and let it terminate smoothly. In Windows, the process is killed explicitly by user. Let's see an example to create an orphan process in Perl.

Script

```
$child=fork;
if($child<0)
{
	print "Parent process ($$)\n";
	sleep 2;
	print "Parent Finished\n";
}
else
{
	print "Child process ($$)\n";
	sleep 3;
	print "Child process ($$) becoming
orphaned\n";
	sleep 2;
	print "Child Finished\n";
}
```

Output

```
G:\Programs\Perl\Process Handling>perl pp7.pl
Parent process (14236)
Child process (-9220)
Parent Finished
Child process (-9220) becoming orphaned
```

```
Child Finished
```

So how to handle orphans? The main problem is because the parent terminates before child. So if we somehow make the parent to halt until the child completes is the solution. This is done by a function called **wait**. Basically what it does is it makes the parent to halt until it receives SIGCHLD signal from all the child created by parent. Let's see the same example but added wait function at the end of if statement.

Script

```
$child=fork;

if($child<0)

{

        print "Parent process ($$)\n";

        sleep 2;

        print "Parent waiting\n";

        wait;

        print "Parent Finished\n";

}

else

{

        print "Child process ($$)\n";

        sleep 5;

        print "Child Finished\n";
```

```
}
```

Output

```
G:\Programs\Perl\Process Handling>perl pp8.pl
Parent process (15576)
Child process (-5764)
Parent waiting
Child Finished
Parent Finished
```

Fork Bomb: There are cases where fork system call may be called indefinitely causing the process to halt in execution and consuming address space. The fork bomb is type of Denial of Service attack. Let's see an example.

Script

```
fork;
fork while(1);
```

Output

```
G:\Programs\Perl\Process Handling>perl pp9.pl
```

The output of the script is indefinite waiting, the execution will not stop until you manually halt it.

Warning don't run the above script on your computer, it may leads forever hanging of your system and may require a restart.

Zombie Process: Zombie process is not a ghost in your system that is going to haunt you, rather it's again a special case where *the child dies long before the parent.* Since the parent is still in execution the address space and process information cannot be removed till the parent completes. Even though the execution of child is completed still it occupying the memory waiting for parent to complete hence lying in a midway zone of being completed and not completed fully, the child is said to be in zombie state. Zombies are living dead, since process exhibits the same character it's named as such.

Script

```
$parent=$$;

$child=fork;

if($child<0)

{

      print "Parent ($$) Executing\n";

      sleep 2;

      $c=kill 0,$child;

      print "Child is zombie now\n" if($c==1);

      sleep 2;

      print "Parent Dead\n";

}

else

{

      print "Child ($$) Executing\n";
```

```
        sleep 1;
        print "Child became zombie\n";
        print "Waiting for parent to die\n";
}
```

Output

```
G:\Programs\Perl\Process Handling>perl pp10.pl
Parent (18204) Executing
Child (-8764) Executing
Child became zombie
Waiting for parent to die
Child is zombie now
Parent Dead
```

Pipes: Pipe is a unidirectional communication channel between two processes. Input is written into one end and read of from other end. The pipe can be of two types *anonymous pipes* which are achieved by using '|' symbol and *named pipes* which are created by functions. Pipes are more flexible under UNIX system to avoid temporary buffers. The following diagram simulates a simple pipe.

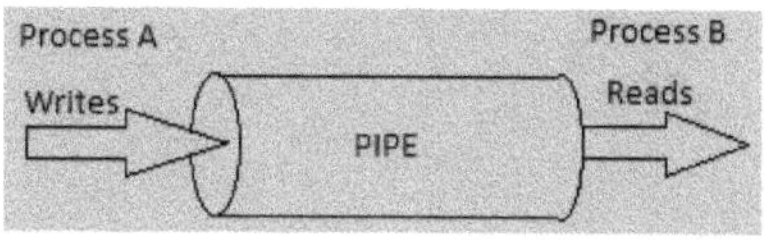

Until now we have seen how to create process, now let's discuss how with the use of these pipes the process communicates.

Anonymous Pipes: These pipes are created by system with output (write) set to STDIN and input (read) set to STDOUT by default. These can be readily executed in command line. Let's see a Windows version of anonymous pipe implementation. For UNIX users, use equivalent UNIX command in place of Windows commands.

Script

```
print "\ndir.txt contains\n";

print "==============================\n";

open(FILE,"<dir.txt") or die "Error:$!\n";

while(<FILE>)

{

      print $_;

}

HERE:close FILE;


print "\nSorted file by date with pipe\n";

print "==============================\n";

open(FILE,"sort dir.txt|") or die "Error:$!\n";

while(<FILE>)

{

      print $_;

}

HERE1:close FILE;
```

Output

```
G:\Programs\Perl\Process Handling>perl pp11.pl

dir.txt contains

=================================

12/20/2015  07:43 PM    <DIR>          .

12/20/2015  07:43 PM    <DIR>          ..

12/20/2015  07:46 PM                 0 dir.txt

12/19/2015  11:32 PM               150 pp1.pl

12/20/2015  12:28 AM               205 pp2.pl

12/20/2015  02:04 AM                58 pp3.pl

12/20/2015  03:56 AM               145 pp4.pl

12/20/2015  11:42 AM               267 pp5.pl


Sorted file by date with pipe

=================================

12/19/2015  11:32 PM               150 pp1.pl

12/20/2015  02:04 AM                58 pp3.pl

12/20/2015  03:56 AM               145 pp4.pl

12/20/2015  07:43 PM    <DIR>          .

12/20/2015  07:43 PM    <DIR>          ..

12/20/2015  07:46 PM                 0 dir.txt

12/20/2015  11:42 AM               267 pp5.pl

12/20/2015  12:28 AM               205 pp2.pl
```

If the pipe symbol specified at the end it mean pipe is opened for read, and if front well it's for write.

Named Pipe: There are drawbacks in anonymous pipes, firstly pipes can only be used on process that have a common lineage like a parent and child process; secondly they are not permanent as they are created on process birth and deleted by process death.

To overcome this deficiency we go for named pipes or otherwise called as FIFO's. They are all way similar to pipe except they are permanent. UNIX treats them as files and its one of the easiest method for process communication. In Windows we don't have any feature or system call to generate FIFO's. Even though **Win32::Pipe** module promises to deliver named pipes, it fails in execution as it's a broken module. Let's hope there will be even better module available in future. But I am not gonna skip the topic here I will discuss the available function and its purpose so that you will be well prepared.

Creation: The module contains new method which can create a pipe and returns a pipe object. The following is the syntax:

```
$namedpipe=new Win32::Pipe(UNC_NAME);
```

The UNC name specifies the place where the named pipe is created. This is generally "\.\pipe\Pipename".

Connection Establishment: The created pipe will start to run in the assigned port, now we instruct server to wait till there is a connection is made, this is done by this command. It blocks the process and run only when the client makes a request for the pipe. The syntax for accepting the connection establishment is:

```
$namedpipe->Connect();
```

Pipe Reads and Writes: The pipe reads and write are simple by calling a function. The reads return the value available in the pipe. The writes takes the parameter that is to be written onto the pipe. The syntax is listed out below:

```
$data=$namedpipe->Read();
```

```
$namedpipe->Write($data);
```

Closing the Pipe: The pipe before closing is disconnected and then terminated. Disconnect is done in server side of script. The syntax is:

```
$namedpipe->Disconnect();
```

```
$namedpipe->Close();
```

Pipe Function: To increase the portability and provide a solution for Windows system, Perl offers this function. The function syntax is:

pipe READ, WRITE

Where READ and WRITE are handles to perform read and write operation. Note while handling with this function it's better to fork almost immediately as possible.

Let's see an example how to read and write through pipe. We use only the print function specifying the handle to perform our task.

Script

```
pipe(PIPE_R,PIPE_W);
STDOUT->autoflush(1);
PIPE_R->autoflush(1);
PIPE_W->autoflush(1);
$child=fork;
if($child<0)
{
	close PIPE_R;
	foreach(1..5)
	{
		print PIPE_W "$_\n";
		print "Parent: $_ \n";
		sleep 1;
	}
	close PIPE_W;
}
else
{
	close PIPE_W;
	foreach(1..5)
	{
		sleep 1;
```

```
            $a=<PIPE_R>;
            print "Child: $a";
        }
        close PIPE_R;
}
```

Output

```
G:\Programs\Perl\Process Handling>perl pp12.pl
Parent: 1
Parent: 2
Child: 1
Child: 2
Parent: 3
Child: 3
Parent: 4
Child: 4
Parent: 5
Child: 5
```

The output may vary from system to system. Thus we established a communication between two processes. Here at start I have use a function called **autoflush** which flushes out data from the buffer on encountering a newline. So only I have used '\n' at end compulsorily on each print. If you don't use "\n" then the parent process will write into the buffer until it is full and then only it's flushed out to the child process. So be careful to do this as your practice.

System V Communication: The UNIX System V users have a lot of methods for interprocess communication such as *Shared Memory, Message Queues* and *Semaphores*, which is more elegant than available in Windows. If you have a UNIX OS on your system run the below code and see the how the processes communicate through a shared memory.

Script

```
$key=0x1000;

$shmid=shmget($key,11,IPC_CREAT|0666);

if($shmid<0){

      print "Error";

      exit(1);}

if(fork<0){

      die "Error $!" if(shmwrite($shmid,"Hello
Gokul",0,11)==0);

      wait; }

else{

      sleep 1;

      die "Error $!" if(shmread($shmid,$msg,
0,11)==0);

      print "Child read from Shared Memory:
$msg\n"; }
```

DATABASE ACCESS

In the beginning of this book, I told Perl is quite famous for its file system access similarly it has a simple way to access database. *Database (DB)* is a set of organized data which is accessed when it is needed in either hierarchical or relational manner. Perl offers many DB drivers such as for *Oracle, SQLite, MySQL* and other familiar DB's.

Refresh your SQL:

Let's learn only the important commands that are required for handling database, so our discussion on this topic would be in short. For those who are not familiar with database I personally recommend to have a keen look to this section and others, well you can skip to part where we use Perl to access database. On advance I inform you that I am going to use *SQLite* database which is an open source and lightweight database.

SQL stands for Structured Query Language. It is a language used for manipulating, storing and retrieving data from the Relational Database. SQL is used in RDBMS (*Relational Data Base Management System*). All RDBMS are implemented via the usage of Relations. Relation are also called as tables which contains collection of rows (*records*) and columns (*fields*).

Some of the RDBMS used are Postgres, Informix, MS access, Oracle, MySQL, Sybase, SQLite...etc.

Note: SQL commands are not case sensitive, but the values inside ' ' are case sensitive. But for readability I have capitalized all the SQL commands. Note while you download sqlite the .exe file name would be'sqlite3' I have renamed it to 'sqlite'.

Creating Database: Database is a collection of tables. To create a new database the following syntax is implied.

```
>sqlite <database_name>
```

Example:

```
G:\Programs\Perl\Database>sqlite Sample.db
```

After this the prompt changes to 'sqlite>'. The database Sample.db is created on the specified directory. Here 'G:\Programs\Perl\Database'.

Creating Table: Tables are basic object in the database. To create a new relation on database the following syntax is implied.

```
>CREATE TABLE <tablename> (<colname1> datatype1
<constraint> ...);
```

Constraint may be of following:

Not Null: This constraints is used to specify that a column may never hold a NULL value.

Default: This constraint provide a default value to column when an INSERT INTO statement does not provide a specific value.

Unique: These constraints ensure that all value in column are distinct and NULL values is accepted.

Primary Key: A primary key is used to uniquely identify each row in a table and also will not allow a NULL value. Primary Key=Unique + Not Null

Example:

```
sqlite>    CREATE    TABLE    Customer    (custid
integer(3) PRIMARY KEY, name varchar(20));
```

Table Description: To view the table description. In other words, it helps us to know about the detailed information about the table.

```
sqlite>.schema <tablename>
```

Example:

```
sqlite> .schema Customer
```

```
CREATE   TABLE   Customer   (custid   integer(3)
PRIMARY KEY, name varchar(20));
```

Modifying Table and Column Definition: To modify the table fields by adding or removing and altering its data types. To modify or delete a column is not possible in SQLite (Possible in other DB's (Oracle)). To add a column

```
ALTER TABLE <tablename> ADD COLUMN <newcolumn>
datatype;
```

Example:

```
sqlite> ALTER TABLE Customer ADD COLUMN phone
varchar(10);
```

```
sqlite> .schema Customer

CREATE TABLE Customer (custid integer(3) PRIMARY KEY, name varchar(20), phone varchar(10));
```

List available tables: To see what tables available in the database, we have a command called

```
sqlite>.tables
```

Example:

```
sqlite> .tables

Customer
```

Deleting Tables: This will permanently remove the table, its schema along with its data permanently. So be careful when you use this command.

```
DROP TABLE <tablename>;
```

Example:

```
sqlite> DROP TABLE Customer;

sqlite> .tables
```

Inserting Data to Table: When adding a new row, we must ensure that the datatype of the value and the column matches the insert of data in relation. The syntax is

```
INSERT INTO <tablename> VALUES (value1 …);
```

Example:

```
sqlite> INSERT INTO Customer VALUES(100,
'Gokul', 1234567890);
```

Viewing the Table Content: As such entering data into the database is of no use. Hence to see what the content of the relation are, SELECT query is used. This is the most often used query in the database. The various forms are:

1) To select entire record from the table

```
SELECT * FROM <table>;
```

2) To select a particular column from the relation

```
SELECT <col> FROM <table>;
```

3) To select multiple column from the relation

```
SELECT <col1>, <col2>… FROM <table>;
```

4) To apply a particular expression to a column without affecting the content of the relation

```
SELECT <col><expr><val> FROM <table>;
```

5) To select only the unique values from the relation

```
SELECT DISTINCT <col1> FROM <table>;
```

6) To select particular columns which is ordered by the column specified in the query

```
SELECT * FROM <table> ORDER BY <column>;
```

7) To select the contents of table with respect to the content of column in query in ascending order

```
SELECT * FROM <table> ORDER BY <column> ASC;
```

8) To select the contents of table with respect to the content of column in query in descending order

```
SELECT * FROM <table> ORDER BY <column> DESC;
```

9)
```
SELECT <column> FROM <table> WHERE
(<condition1> OR <condition2>);
```

10)
```
SELECT <column> FROM <table> WHERE
(<condition1> AND <condition2>);
```

11)
```
SELECT <column> FROM <table> WHERE <col> IN
(<val1>, <val2>…);
```

12)
```
SELECT <column> FROM <table> WHERE <col>
BETWEEN <val1> AND <val2>;
```

Example:

```
sqlite> SELECT * FROM Customer;

100|Gokul|1234567890

101|Mythili|9087654321

102|Pandian|1029384756
```

We can modify the way of displaying content by adding header by using following commands.

```
sqlite> .header on

sqlite> .mode column
```

Now after these commands when we try to view the table this, we get:

```
sqlite> SELECT * FROM Customer;

custid      name        phone
----------  ----------  ----------
100         Gokul       1234567890
101         Mythili     9087654321
102         Pandian     1029384756
```

<u>Updating Table:</u> The update statement is used to modify the content of the relation contained in the database. The update can either be of Tuple (row) or Column update.

1) UPDATE <table> SET <col1>=<val1>, <col2>=<val2>… [WHERE clause]

2) UPDATE <table> SET <col>=<val> [WHERE clause]

Example:

```
sqlite> SELECT * FROM Customer;

custid      name        phone
----------  ----------  ----------
100         Gokul       1234567890
101         Mythili     9087654321
102         Pandian     1029384756

sqlite> UPDATE Customer SET custid=custid+100;
```

```
sqlite> SELECT * FROM Customer;
custid      name        phone
----------  ----------  ----------
200         Gokul       1234567890
201         Mythili     9087654321
202         Pandian     1029384756
```

<u>Deleting row of table:</u> The rows of table can be deleted, through this query.

```
DELETE FROM <table> [WHERE clause]
```

Example:

```
sqlite> SELECT * FROM Customer;
custid      name        phone
----------  ----------  ----------
200         Gokul       1234567890
201         Mythili     9087654321
202         Pandian     1029384756
305         Lavanya     147258369

sqlite> DELETE FROM Customer WHERE custid=305;

sqlite> SELECT * FROM Customer;
```

```
custid      name        phone
----------  ----------  ----------
200         Gokul       1234567890
201         Mythili     9087654321
202         Pandian     1029384756
```

SQLite Datatypes: SQLite offers the following datatypes: Integer, Varchar, Real/Float, Blob (Binary large object to store images and such files), character and date.

Now that we have learnt enough to handle the database, now we learn how to perform all this manual operation through programming. Before so, let's see the architecture of how Perl access the database.

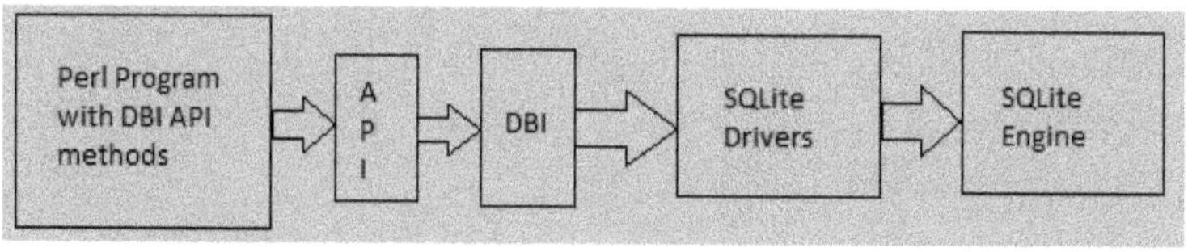

The API (Application Programming Interface) defines the interface for call of methods and variables for Perl script to use. This is implemented by DBI.

The DBI communicates with the method calls to direct where the actual execution for the appropriate driver exists.

Each driver are implemented with complex interface functions and other database operations. Then the drivers instruct the respective engine to perform the required task. This is the basic operation underlying in these architectures. Now let's gets into scripting.

Module used: From the architecture itself you must have guessed it. The **DBI** module serves for database programming.

Connection Establishment: The DBI module contain a method called **connect** which serves this purpose. The formal way to call this function is:

```
$con=DBI->connect($driver,$username,$password);
```

The driver is specified as 'DBI:<database>:<userdbname>'. For our discussion using SQLite, we have to use 'DBI:SQLite:Sample.db' (make sure Sample.db is same directory as the Perl script). For other database we require username and password, but in SQLite there is no username and password.

Query Creation: The SQL commands (such as CREATE, INSERT) are specified in this function. It prepares the query for execution. The method call is:

```
$stmt=DBI->prepare($query);
```

Query Execution: The prepare SQL query is executed by passing it to the SQLite Engine which is the job of this method. The call to this method is:

```
$stmt->execute();
```

Fetching the data: The resultant data from the table after execution can be fetched in two ways: either as an indexed array or as a hash with key as the column name. Note for each call of this function will move one row down through the result table. The function call is:

1) For array indexing:

```
@row=$stmt->fetchrow_array();
```

The accessing is done as $row[0], $row[1], …

2) For hashing technique:

```
$row=$stmt->fetchrow_hashref();
```

The accessing is done as $$row{'<colname>'}.

Number of rows: To know how many rows are there in the resultant table, DBI has a variable which is set on calling execute method.

```
$nrows=$stmt->rows;
```

Releasing the Executed Result: The variable used in the preparation occupies a large amount of space. For a better and optimized programming, we need to release the variable which is done through this function.

```
$stmt->finish();
```

Database Error identifier: During any of above operation there is a chance of error raise which is handled by using error handling mechanism to safely terminate the script. But to know the exact detail about the error we have a facility, by using following statement.

```
$err=DBI::errstr;
```

Now let's see a fully-fledged code to list out the data contained in the table.

Script

```
use DBI;
```

```
my $dbcon= DBI->connect("DBI:SQLite:Sample.db",
'','') or die "Error ",$DBI::errstr,"\n";

my $stmt= $dbcon->prepare("SELECT * FROM
Customer");

$stmt->execute() or die "Error ",
$DBI::errstr,"\n";

while(my $row=$stmt->fetchrow_hashref())

{

      my ($id,$name) = ($$row{'custid'},
$$row{'name'});

      print "Id: $id\tName: $name\n";

}

print "Number of rows found is ",$stmt->rows;

$stmt->finish();
```

Output

```
G:\Programs\Perl\Database>perl pd1.pl

Id: 200 Name: Gokul

Id: 201 Name: Mythili

Id: 202 Name: Pandian

Number of rows found is 3
```

In the previous program we used the hashing technique, if the same program to rewritten in array indexing method, the loop changes as

```
while(my @row=$stmt->fetchrow_array())

{

	my ($id,$name) = ($row[0], $row[1]);

	print "Id: $id\tName: $name\n";

}
```

Now let's see an example to insert a value into the table. The same program is used but the query preparation varies.

Script

```
use DBI;

my $dbcon= DBI-
>connect("DBI:SQLite:Sample.db",'','') or die
"Error ",$DBI::errstr,"\n";

my $stmt= $dbcon->prepare("SELECT * FROM
Customer");

$stmt->execute() or die "Error
",$DBI::errstr,"\n";

while(my @row=$stmt->fetchrow_array())

{

	my ($id,$name) = ($row[0], $row[1]);

	print "Id: $id\tName: $name\n";

}

print "Number of rows found is ".$stmt-
>rows."\n";
```

```
$stmt->finish();


$stmt= $dbcon->prepare("INSERT INTO Customer
VALUES(305,\'Lavanya\',\'147258369\')");

$stmt->execute() or die "Error
",$DBI::errstr,"\n";

$stmt->finish();


$stmt= $dbcon->prepare("SELECT * FROM
Customer");

$stmt->execute() or die "Error
",$DBI::errstr,"\n";

while(my @row=$stmt->fetchrow_array())

{

      my ($id,$name) = ($row[0], $row[1]);

      print "Id: $id\tName: $name\n";

}

print "Number of rows found is ",$stmt->rows;

$stmt->finish();
```

Output

```
G:\Programs\Perl\Database>perl pd3.pl

Id: 200 Name: Gokul

Id: 201 Name: Mythili

Id: 202 Name: Pandian
```

```
Number of rows found is 3

Id: 200 Name: Gokul

Id: 201 Name: Mythili

Id: 202 Name: Pandian

Id: 305 Name: Lavanya

Number of rows found is 4
```

Wildcard Entries:

In the previous program we inserted a value to table which is by default and if you want to insert any other value you have to change the values at this place. This is not an example of good programming. So to improve the scalability of our code we add wildcard entries to our program. They are represented by '?'. In run time the '?' are replaced by values.

Let's see a sample code of how to deal with wildcards.

Script

```
use DBI;

my $dbcon= DBI-
>connect("DBI:SQLite:Sample.db",'','') or die
"Error ",$DBI::errstr,"\n";

my $stmt= $dbcon->prepare("SELECT * FROM
Customer");

$stmt->execute() or die "Error
",$DBI::errstr,"\n";

while(my @row=$stmt->fetchrow_array())
```

```
{
      my ($id,$name) = ($row[0], $row[1]);
      print "Id: $id\tName: $name\n";
}
print "Number of rows found is ".$stmt-
>rows."\n\n";
$stmt->finish();


$stmt= $dbcon->prepare("INSERT INTO Customer
VALUES(?,?,?)");
print "Enter Customer Id:\t";
chomp($custid=<STDIN>);
print "Enter Name of Customer:\t";
chomp($name=<STDIN>);
print "Enter Phone number of customer:\t";
chomp($phn=<STDIN>);
$stmt->execute($custid,$name,"$phn") or die
"Error ",$DBI::errstr,"\n";
$stmt->finish();
$stmt= $dbcon->prepare("SELECT * FROM
Customer");
$stmt->execute() or die "Error
",$DBI::errstr,"\n";
while(my @row=$stmt->fetchrow_array())
{
```

```
      my ($id,$name) = ($row[0], $row[1]);
      print "\nId: $id\tName: $name";
}
print "\nNumber of rows found is ",$stmt->rows;
$stmt->finish();
```

Output

```
G:\Programs\Perl\Database>perl pd4.pl
Id: 200 Name: Gokul
Id: 201 Name: Mythili
Id: 202 Name: Pandian
Id: 305 Name: Lavanya
Number of rows found is 4

Enter Customer Id:      309
Enter Name of Customer: Hariprasath
Enter Phone number of customer: 963258741

Id: 200 Name: Gokul
Id: 201 Name: Mythili
Id: 202 Name: Pandian
Id: 305 Name: Lavanya
Id: 309 Name: Hariprasath
Number of rows found is 5
```

Can you see the changes I made in this script compared to the previous script? There are notably two important changes made. They are

```
$stmt= $dbcon->prepare("INSERT INTO Customer
VALUES(?,?,?)");
```

and

```
$stmt->execute($custid,$name,"$phn") or die
"Error ",$DBI::errstr,"\n";
```

The execute function takes as many parameters as there are '?' in the prepare function. The order of parameter in execute should match the order specified in prepare.

Let see another example with wild card to fetch a particular record from the table.

Script

```
use DBI;

my $dbcon= DBI-
>connect("DBI:SQLite:Sample.db",'','') or die
"Error ",$DBI::errstr,"\n";

my $stmt= $dbcon->prepare("SELECT * FROM
Customer WHERE custid = ?");

$stmt->execute() or die "Error
",$DBI::errstr,"\n";

print "Enter ID of Customer:\t";

$custid=<STDIN>;

$stmt->execute($custid) or die "Error
",$DBI::errstr,"\n";
```

```
@row=$stmt->fetchrow_array();
if($stmt->rows==1)
{
      print "Customer ID: ".$row[0];
      print "\nCustomer Name: ".$row[1];
      print "\nCustomer Phone No: ".$row[2];
}
elsif($stmt->rows>1)
{
      print "Duplicates are found!! Please
check database";
}
else
{
      print "No records Found";
}
$stmt->finish();
```

Output

```
G:\Programs\Perl\Database>perl pd5.pl
Enter ID of Customer:   200
Customer ID: 200
Customer Name: Gokul
Customer Phone No: 1234567890
```

Faster Execution: Some queries are simple success or failure queries which does not require any preparing and execution separately such as CREATE, INSERT and DELETE. In such cases we can directly execute using this function:

```
$con->do($query);
```

Script

```
use DBI;

my $dbcon= DBI->connect("DBI:SQLite:Sample.db",
'','') or die "Error ",$DBI::errstr,"\n";

$dbcon->do("CREATE TABLE Sample(value
integer(3))") or die "Error",$DBI::errstr,"\n";

$dbcon->do("INSERT INTO Sample VALUES(1)") or
die "Error",$DBI::errstr,"\n";

$dbcon->do("INSERT INTO Sample VALUES(2)") or
die "Error",$DBI::errstr,"\n";

$stmt=$dbcon->prepare("SELECT * FROM Sample");

$stmt->execute() or die "Error
",$DBI::errstr,"\n";

while(my @row=$stmt->fetchrow_array())

{     print $row[0]."\t";     }

print "\n"; sleep 20;

$dbcon->do("DROP TABLE Sample") or die
"Error",$DBI::errstr,"\n";
```

Output

```
G:\Programs\Perl\Database>perl pd6.pl

1       2
```

SYSTEM INFORMATION

Some specific application may require information that are contained by the operating system, which includes user name, time of the day and so on. Let's take a look at each information that are necessary.

User of the System: There are cases where the application may require user data such as user name, user id and group id. For such cases we have function inbuilt in Perl to access these valuable information and not irritate the user to enter these details. Let's take a look of how to access them.

Script

```
#Get the current user name

print "The current user logged onto the system
is ",getlogin;

print "\nThe real user id $<";

print "\nThe effective user id $>";

print "\nThe real group id $(";

print "\nThe effective group id $)";
```

Output

```
G:\Programs\Perl\SystemInformation>perl ps1.pl

The current user logged onto the system is
Gokul Amuthan

The real user id 0

The effective user id 0
```

```
The real group id 0

The effective group id 0
```

Now to obtain the detailed information we have a module called **Win32::pwent** which serves this purpose. This module is not available as default, it's downloaded from cpan, using following the following command.

```
cpan Win32::pwent
```

Make sure you have a working internet connection and be patient until module installs, never close the command prompt until the control is returned to you. If you have successfully installed the module the following script works.

Script

```
use Win32;

use Win32::pwent "getpwnam";


print "User name is ",(getpwnam(getlogin))[0];

print "\nNumerical user ID is
",(getpwnam(getlogin))[2];

print "\nNumerical primary group ID is
",(getpwnam(getlogin))[3];

print "\nUser's disk storage limit in KB is
",(getpwnam(getlogin))[4];

print "\nUser's full name is
",(getpwnam(getlogin))[6];
```

```
print "\nUser's default login shell interpreter
is ",(getpwnam(getlogin))[8];
```

Output

```
G:\Programs\Perl\SystemInformation>perl ps5.pl

User name is Gokul Amuthan

Numerical user ID is 1001

Numerical primary group ID is 513

User's disk storage limit in KB is 4294967295

User's full name is Gokul Amuthan.S

User's default login shell interpreter is
C:\WINDOWS\system32\cmd.exe
```

Now for listing all the available users in the system the following script is used.

Script

```
use Win32;

use Win32::pwent "getpwent";


$i=0;

while(($a,$b,$c,$d,$e,$f,$g)=(getpwent)[0..7])

{

      print "\n\nUser ",$i+1;

      print "\nUser name: ",$a;

      print "\nPassword(encrpted): ",$b;
```

```
        print "\nUser ID: ",$c;
        print "\nGroup ID: ",$d;
        print "\nDisk space(in KB): ",$e;
        if($f)
        {       print "\nComments: ",$f;       }
        else
        {       print  "\nComments:  User  defined
account not mentioned the purpose of it"; }
        if($g)
        {       print "\nFull name of user: ",$g; }
        else
        {       print "\nFull name of user: ",$a; }
        $i++;
}
```

Output

```
G:\Programs\Perl\SystemInformation>perl ps6.pl


User 1
User name: Administrator
Password(encrpted):
User ID: 500
Group ID: 513
Disk space(in KB): 4294967295
```

Comments: Built-in account for administering the computer/domain

Full name of user: Administrator

User 2

User name: Gokul Amuthan

Password(encrpted):

User ID: 1001

Group ID: 513

Disk space(in KB): 4294967295

Comments: User defined account not mentioned the purpose of it

Full name of user: Gokul Amuthan.S

Now to get the username of particular user given that you have the group id the following script is quite useful.

Script

```
use Win32;

use Win32::pwent qw(getgrgid getgrnam);


print ((getgrgid(513))[3]);

print "Bad Information"
unless(getgrnam(getgrgid(513))==513);
```

Output

```
G:\Programs\Perl\SystemInformation>perl ps7.pl

Administrator Guest Gokul Amuthan
DefaultAccount
```

Alternate way of the above code is as follows:

Script

```
use Win32;

use Win32::pwent "getgrent";


while (($name,$member)=(getgrent())[0,3])

{

      print "$name ",($member=~ s/ /,/g)+1,"
has members.\nThey are $member\n\n";

}
```

Output

```
G:\Programs\Perl\SystemInformation>perl ps8.pl

None 5 has members.

They are Administrator,
Guest,Gokul,Amuthan,DefaultAccount
```

These are the important functions that are available in the **Win32::pwent** module. It may come in use when you write a Perl script to create a log file in the system.

<u>**System Time:**</u> The time and date in Perl are calculated based on epoch time value which is January 1, 1970. This value is calculated from the a 32 bit counter that ticks inside your computer forever, in 32bit system there arises a problem where the counter eventually runs out and end of time is attained, which is exactly Jan 19, 2038 at 03:14:07 (For more reads about this problem refer sites as 2038 problem).

The functions available in Perl to obtain time are **localtime** and **gmtime**. The localtime function returns the time in the current time zone whereas the gmtime function returns the GMT time zone. For these two function **time** function is passed as a parameter. The time function returns the epoch value.

The return value of locatime and gmtime function is of the form:

1) sec, seconds of minutes from 0 to 59

2) min, minutes of hour from 0 to 59

3) hour, hours of day from 0 to 24

4) mday, day of month from 1 to 31

5) mon, month of year from 0 to 11

6) year, year since 1900

7) wday, days since sunday

8) yday, days since January 1st

9) isdst, hours of daylight savings time

Script

```
@months = qw( Jan Feb Mar Apr May Jun Jul Aug
Sep Oct Nov Dec );

@days = qw(Sun Mon Tue Wed Thu Fri Sat Sun);

($sec,$min,$hour,$mday,$mon,$year,$wday,$yday,$
isdst) = localtime();

print "$mday $months[$mon] $days[$wday]
",1900+$year;

printf(" %.2d:%.2d:%.2d",$hour,$min,$sec);

print "\n$yday passed in this year\n";

$isdst?print "Daylight saving is on":print
"Daylight saving is off";
```

Output

```
G:\Programs\Perl\SystemInformation>perl ps2.pl

24 Dec Thu 2015 01:01:45

357 passed in this year

Daylight saving is off
```

Now let's see how to these complications and print us the required value in ease. The conversion written above are

Script

```
print "Local time is ",scalar localtime time;

print "\nGMT time is ",scalar gmtime time;

print "\nNumber of seconds from 1st Jan 1900 is
",time;
```

Output

```
G:\Programs\Perl\SystemInformation>perl ps3.pl

Local time is Thu Dec 24 01:10:47 2015

GMT time is Wed Dec 23 19:40:47 2015

Number of seconds from 1st Jan 1900 is
1450900099
```

Password Encryption: What is a system without any encryption mechanism for important messages and password? Even if it's available, it's not accessible for the users. For user purpose Perl offers an encryption function which provides a good encryption as the system does. The **crypt** function serves this purpose. This function takes two parameters; one the original text and another a passphrase called salt. There is no separate decryption function available in Perl but if you are familiar with encryption mechanism, using result from the encryption mechanism we can use for checking the original message is correct or not. You might be confused by above statement, let's see an example of how the crypt function can be used.

Script

```
#Password encryption

$realpwd='Gokul';

$salt='Perl In Your Hands';

$encrypt=crypt $realpwd,$salt;

while(1)
```

```
{
      print "Enter the password:\t";
      $pwd=<STDIN>;
      chomp $pwd;
      $decrypt=crypt $pwd,$encrypt;
      exit if($encrypt eq $decrypt);
      print "\nOOPS!!!Wrong password Retry in 2 seconds............\n";
      sleep 2;
      system "cls";
}
```

Output

```
G:\Programs\Perl\SystemInformation>perl ps9.pl
Enter the password:     Gokul
```

CPU Execution Time: The **times** function helps to return the amount of time used by the CPU for a particular process. This function returns four elements; user time, system time, child time, child system time. Since all the execution happens in milliseconds for normal script you can't see much difference.

Not to be confused with **time** both can be used for calculation but **times** offers better value than time function which always rounds off.

Let's take a look how this function works.

Script

```
$child=fork;

($su,$ss)=times;

$a=0;

if($child<0)

{

	for(1..10000000)

	{

	$a**=($a+$_**$_**$_**$_**$_)**($a+$_**$_*
*$_**$_**$_);

	}

	sleep 10;

	($eu,$es)=times;

	print "For process $$\n";

	print "For 10000000 calculations user
time taken is ",$eu-$su," seconds\n";

	print "For 10000000 calculations system
time taken is ",$es-$ss," seconds\n";

	wait;

}

else

{

	for(1..100000000)
```

```
      {

      $a**=($a+$_**$_**$_**$_**$_)**($a+$_**$_*
*$_**$_**$_);

      }

      ($eu,$es)=times;

      print "For process $$\n";

      print "For 100000000 calculations user
time taken is ",$eu-$su," seconds\n";

      print "For 100000000 calculations system
time taken is ",$es-$ss," seconds\n";

}
```

Output

```
G:\Programs\Perl\SystemInformation>perl ps11.pl

For process 6124

For 10000000 calculations user time taken is
28.39 seconds

For 10000000 calculations system time taken is
0.015 seconds

For process -452

For 100000000 calculations user time taken is
102.468 seconds

For 100000000 calculations system time taken is
0.031 seconds
```

Halting the CPU:

The sleep function halts the execution for specified amount of time. The sleeping time is not reflected on times function. But in last program is reflected how? It's because even though parent was sleeping, child still used the CPU so the sleep time was reflected.

Sleep function always specified in integer value, now for non-integer values of sleep, we can use the **select** function, by specifying three undef values and non-integer value as the last parameter.

The following script shows the usage of non-integer timed sleep.

Script

```
#Sleep and Select

print "Sleep function\n";

$st=time;

sleep 5;

$et=time;

print "Time slept=",$et-$st;

print "\nSelect function\n";

$st=time;

select undef,undef,undef,3.5;

$et=time;

print "Time slept=",$et-$st;
```

Output

```
G:\Programs\Perl\SystemInformation>perl ps15.pl
Sleep function
Time slept=5
Select function
Time slept=4
```

Since we used the time function the values is rounded off.

Environment Variables: The Environment variable of the system can be printed using the inbuilt variable of Perl called **%ENV**. Let's see an example script of how to access. Note don't try to change this variable it may result in unwanted behavior.

Script

```
#Environment variables
$path=$ENV{PATH};
$path=~ s/;;|;/\n/g;
print "The path variable contains\n",$path;
```

Output (Reduced in size of data printed)

```
G:\Programs\Perl\SystemInformation>perl ps16.pl
The path variable contains
C:\Perl64\site\bin
```

NETWORKING

Networking is a wide area in computer science and it's not possible to master it as such. Perl offers better networking facility than C. It's much simple and easy to create a client-server model. Before going deep let's get some knowledge of how the networking concept. Irrespective of the system you are using, every system consists of seven important layers; Presentation, Application, Session, Transport, Network, Data Link and Physical Layer. The communication between each layer is governed by a mechanism called protocol. There are two types: *TCP/IP* and *UDP*.

TCP/IP is a connection oriented protocol whereas UDP is connectionless hence unreliable. The two node in a network communicated through ports and sockets that are available. Each node is allocated with a unique id called IP address. One of the special IP address is 127.0.0.1 called as loopback address which represent the current system. Let's limit our discussion to creating and communicating with sockets. Before going into socket creation, let's get an idea how to obtain network information.

Network Information: To establish a connection between the systems, we first need to know some basic information about the system such as its IP address and/or host name. For these purpose Perl offers some inbuilt function that serves this purpose.

To get host information by using the host name, we have a function **gethostbyname** which returns the host name, alias name, Address type, Address length and IP address.

Script

```
#Host details by name
print "\nEnter a host name:\t";
chomp($host=<STDIN>);
if($host=~/[A-Z][a-z]|./)
{
	($name,$aliases,$addrtype,$length,@addres
s)=gethostbyname $host;
	if($name)
	{
		print "\nHost Name: $name";
		print "\nAliases Name: $aliases";
		print "\nAddress type: $addrtype";
		print "\nLength of address:
$length";
	$address=join('.',unpack("C4",scalar
gethostbyname($host)));
		print "\nAddress(with unpacking):
$address";
	}
	else
	{	print "Host not found"; }
```

```
}
else
{     print "Enter a valid entry";  }
```

Output

```
J:\Perl\Networking>perl pn1.pl
Enter a host name:      Gokul
Host Name: Gokul
Aliases Name:
Address type: 2
Length of address: 4
Address(with unpacking): 127.0.0.1
```

There is a new function in the above script which is **unpack**, which the reverse operation of **pack** function. What pack function does is, that is converts the supplied string to a specified format. In our example the IP address is octets and so we use 'C' and there are four of them so we used '4'.

Now let's see an example of how to do the reverse process that is having an IP address to get information of host.

Script

```
use IO::Socket::INET;
use Data::VString "parse_vstring";
```

```
#Host detail by address
print "\nEnter host ip address:\t";
chomp($ip=<STDIN>);
if($ip=~/[0-9]|./)
{
	$a=($ip=~tr/././);
	$ip=parse_vstring($ip);
	if($a==3)
	{
		$name=gethostbyaddr $ip,AF_INET;
		if($name)
		{	print "Hostname: $name"; }
		else
		{	print "Host not found"; }
	}
	else
	{	goto b;	}
}
else
{
	b:	print "Enter a valid ip";
}
```

Output

```
G:\Programs\Perl\Networking>perl pn2.pl

Enter host ip address:  192.168.252.1

Hostname: Gokul.mshome.net
```

In the previous script the module **Data::VString** is not available as default, which installed from cpan.org. Another way of doing the above process is to use **inet** functions. The following is the script is implementation of the inet function.

Script

```
use Socket;


$ip=inet_aton("www.google.com");

print "The IP Address of www.google.com is: ".inet_ntoa($ip);

print "\n\nAddress constants";

print "\nINADDR_NONE is: ".inet_ntoa (INADDR_NONE);

print "\nINADDR_ANY is: ".inet_ntoa (INADDR_ANY);

print "\nINADDR_LOOPBACK is: ".inet_ntoa (INADDR_LOOPBACK);

print "\nINADDR_BROADCAST is: ".inet_ntoa (INADDR_BROADCAST);
```

Output

```
G:\Programs\Perl\Networking>perl pn3.pl

The IP Address of www.google.com is:
74.125.239.52


Address constants

INADDR_NONE is: 255.255.255.255

INADDR_ANY is: 0.0.0.0

INADDR_LOOPBACK is: 127.0.0.1

INADDR_BROADCAST is: 255.255.255.255
```

The above program apart from the IP information contains predefined constants used in special cases such as representing current machine we use INADDR_LOOPBACK instead of typing 127.0.0.1 which is hard to remember.

This is not the end to information about the host that can be gathered, there are much more but these are the most important function that you should know to create a simple networking application. Now that the basics are over, let's learn to create a simple socket program.

Socket: The Socket programming creates an environment to communicate between two machines. This is provided by **Socket** module in Perl. The socket structure is returned by the function **sockaddr_in** which takes two arguments PORT and ADDRESS. This also performs the reverse operation to extract the information in different context if the parameter is of the type SOCKADDR_IN.

Before getting to creation of sockets let's see an overview of how the sockets work. The socket is initially started at the server machine, which *bind*s and *listen*s for client's request. If a client *connect*s to that particular socket, the server *accept*s and the communication takes place. After the communication is over the socket is closed. The following is a simple flowchart of the above described process:

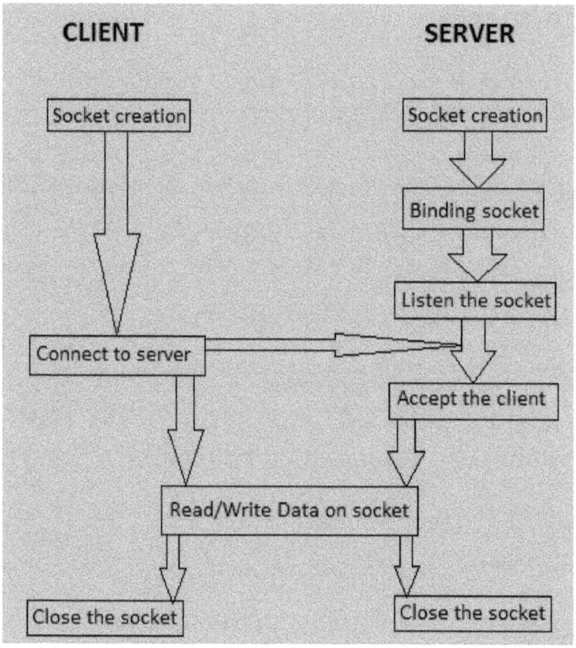

Now let's see each part of the process with its respective function in Perl. The **Socket** module contains all the needed function to implement this.

Socket Creation: The creation is similar in both side. This is done by **socket** function. It takes the form **socket(SOCKET_HANDLE, SOCKET_TYPE, PROTOCOL);** The SOCKET_HANDLE is similar to FILEHANDLE and can be accessed in same manner. The SOCKET_TYPE can hold either of two values SOCK_STREAM for connection oriented mechanism and SOCK_DGRAM for connectionless mechanism. The PROTOCOL also changes respectively as TCP for connection oriented mechanism and UDP for connectionless mechanism. But these are no constants so the **getprotobyname** function is used to return the protocol format.

```
socket(SOCKET,PF_IFNET,SOCK_STREAM,
(getprotobyname('tcp'))[2]);
```

Binding Socket: The socket binding is done at the server side to attach the newly created socket to a local IP address and service port. The Perl function is **bind(SOCKET_HANDLE, SOCKADDR_IN);**

The SOCKADDR_IN format is returned by function **pack_sockaddr_in($PORT,inet_aton($HOSTNAME));** The PORT number can be any value between 1025 and 65535.

```
bind(SOCKET,pack_sockaddr_in($port,
inet_aton($host)));
```

Listen Socket: The listening is a mechanism where the socket is configured to listen for the clients who are ready to connect. There can be 'n' listening at a time that is server can listen to 'n' clients at a time. The first listened client is responded first. To maintain this integrity, the server maintains a FIFO queue to store all the client request. The Perl function is **listen(SOCKET_HANDLE, $NUM);** where NUM represents the number of clients to listen at a time.

```
listen(SOCKET,2);
```

Connecting the server: The client connects to the server though the **connect** method. The connect method helps to place the request in the server queue. The function call to connect is **connect(SOCKET_HANDLE, SOCKADDR_IN);** The SOCKADDR_IN is similar as in bind function.

```
connect(SOCKET,pack_sockaddr_in($port,
inet_aton($host)));
```

Accepting the client: The request from client is accepted by the server using this method. This method blocks the server making it to wait to accept the client request. The function call is **accept(NEW_SOCKET_HANDLE, SOCKET_HANDLE);** The NEW_SOCKET_HANDLE contains the handle for client.

```
accept(NEWSOCKET,SOCKET);
```

Reading and Writing Socket: The reading and writing can be done using the print function in the form **print HANDLE $MESSAGE;**

Closing the Socket: Closing of socket is mandatory, after the process is over. The function used is **close SOCKET_HANDLE;**

```
close SOCKET;
```

These are the function used to create a socket and establish a data connection between the server and client. Now let's see a full-fledged example.

Script

server.pl

```
use Socket;

if($ARGV[0] eq "-h")

{

      print "Usage: server.pl <host> <port>";

}

if(@ARGV==2)

{

      $host=$ARGV[0];

      $port=$ARGV[1];

}

else

{

      $port=1234;

      $host="localhost";

}

socket(SOCKET,PF_IFNET,SOCK_STREAM,(getprotobyn
ame('tcp'))[2])

      or die "Error cant open socket:
".$!."\n";

bind(SOCKET,pack_sockaddr_in($port,inet_aton($h
ost)))
```

```
      or die "Error cant bind socket:
".$!."\n";
listen(SOCKET,2)
      or die "Error cant listen socket:
".$!."\n";
print "Server Started........\n";
print "Listening Socket......\n";
$server_start=time;
while(1)
{
      $diff=$time - $server_start;
      goto HERE if($diff>10);
      if($client=accept(NEWSOCKET,SOCKET))
      {
            print "Client connected..\n";
            $val=scalar localtime;
            $time=time;
            print NEWSOCKET $val;
            close NEWSOCKET;
      }
}
HERE: close SOCKET;
```

client.pl

```
use Socket;

if($ARGV[0] eq "-h")

{

      print "Usage: server.pl <host> <port>";

}

if(@ARGV==2)

{

      $host=$ARGV[0];

      $port=$ARGV[1];

}

else

{

      $port=1234;

      $host="localhost";

}

socket(SOCKET,PF_IFNET,SOCK_STREAM,(getprotobyn
ame('tcp'))[2])

      or die "Error cant open socket:
".$!."\n";

connect(SOCKET,pack_sockaddr_in($port,inet_aton
($host)))

      or die "Error cant connect socket:
".$!."\n";
```

```
print "Connected to server...\n";
$val=<SOCKET>;
print "The time is ".$val."\n";
close SOCKET;
```

<u>Output</u>

server.pl

```
G:\Programs\Perl\Networking>perl server.pl
Server Started........
Listening Socket......
Client connected..
```

client.pl

```
G:\Programs\Perl\Networking>perl client.pl
Connected to server...
The time is Sun Dec 27 03:26:48 2015


G:\Programs\Perl\Networking>perl client.pl
Error cant connect socket: No connection could be made because the target machine actively refused it.
```

Since a timer is set on server after ten seconds the server shuts off by closing the socket and hence on the second client request the client receive a 'No connection' error.

If auto flush has to be set in previous program insert **`$|=1;`** at the start of code on both sides.

The previous program has a facility to write into the client socket only. This may be useful in application such as Date server where the client need not have to reply. But while implementing a chat server, in those cases we require communication on both sides. To do so we have another module called **IO::Socket::INET** which has facility to communicate with server. Let's see the implementation required for this module.

This module offers easy way to set all the functionality on creation itself that is the creation, bind and listen mechanism is combined in same function as socket object creation. Let's see how to create a socket object for server:

```
$socket = new IO::Socket::INET (

LocalHost => HOST_IP_ADDRESS,

LocalPort => PORT,

Proto => PROTOCOL,

Listen => NUM,

Reuse => 1);
```

The socket object for client is:

```
$socket = new IO::Socket::INET (

PeerHost => HOST_IP_ADDRESS,

PeerPort => PORT,

Proto => PROTOCOL);
```

The accept method called using the socket object as,

```
$client_socket = $socket->accept();
```

Separate connect method is not needed in client as the creation of socket object itself perform it. Now the data sending is handled using send and receive methods of form:

```
$client_socket->send($data);
```

And during receive:

```
$data = <$client_socket>;

$client_socket->recv($data,BUFFER_SIZE);
```

The socket closing procedure is same as:

```
$socket->close();
```

This module offers shorter and easier way to script code. Now let's see a fully-fledged script.

Script

server1.pl

```
use IO::Socket::INET;


$|=1;

$socket = new IO::Socket::INET (

LocalHost => '127.0.0.1', LocalPort => '5000',
Proto => 'tcp', Listen => 5,  Reuse => 1)

      or die "ERROR in Socket Creation : $!\n";
```

```
print "SERVER Waiting for client connection on
port 5000\n";

$server_start=time;

while(1)

{

	$time=time;

	$diff=$time - $server_start;

	goto HERE if($diff>10);

	$client_socket = $socket->accept();

	print "Accepted New Client Connection
\n";

	$data = "DATA from Server";

	print $client_socket "$data\n";

	$client_socket->send($data);

	$data = <$client_socket>;

	$client_socket->recv($data,1024);

	print "Received from Client : $data\n";

}

HERE: $socket->close();
```

client1.pl

```
use IO::Socket::INET;


$| = 1;

$socket = new IO::Socket::INET (
```

```
PeerHost => '127.0.0.1', PeerPort => '5000',
Proto => 'tcp')
      or die "ERROR in Socket Creation : $!\n";
print "TCP Connection Success.\n";
$data = <$socket>;
$socket->recv($data,1024);
print "Received from Server : $data\n";
$data = "DATA from Client";
print $socket "$data\n";
$socket->send($data);
$socket->close();
```

<u>Output</u>

server1.pl

```
G:\Programs\Perl\Networking>perl server1.pl
SERVER Waiting for client connection on port
5000
Accepted New Client Connection
Received from Client : DATA from Client
Accepted New Client Connection
Received from Client : DATA from Client
```

client1.pl

```
G:\Programs\Perl\Networking>perl client1.pl
TCP Connection Success.
```

```
Received from Server : DATA from Server


G:\Programs\Perl\Networking>perl client1.pl

TCP Connection Success.

Received from Server : DATA from Server


G:\Programs\Perl\Networking>perl client1.pl

ERROR in Socket Creation : No connection could
be made because the target machine actively
refused it.
```

As discussed in the previous example the server shutdown on timeout and if a client request after time out it receives a ‘Connection Error’. Note that here I have used the $| variable to flush out data immediately. In this it’s important because the server has to flush out immediately to send a response to client and vice versa.

USER INTERFACE DESIGN

What is a language without a good graphical interface? Perl offers one such intriguing user interface, much more flexible and smooth. The look and feel of the interface are much stupendous than in C. Why GUI? Working in terminal requires knowledge of the escape sequence to format the output on screen and it can be very plain. To provide an ease of access for the end users, User Interfaces are developed. The **Tkx** module contains the facility for GUI design for Windows system and **Tk** for UNIX system. Let's see how to design basic object on GUI such as window, frame, button, text box, label, radio button, check box, menu and list.

Window: A window is a basic layout for all the components to be placed. The first window that appear on screen is said to be main or primary window. The following script will create a blank window with title "Hello" and of size 300 x 300.

Script

```
use Tkx;

#Creating Window

$mw=Tkx::widget->new(".");

$mw->g_wm_title("Hello");

$mw->g_wm_minsize(300,300);

$mw->g_wm_resizable(1,1);

Tkx::MainLoop();
```

Output

```
G:\Programs\Perl\GUI>perl pg1.pl
```

The function **g_wm_resizable** allows the window to be resized if it contain parameter 1 and fixed for 0. The function **Tkx::MainLoop()** is event job that repeatedly calls the script forever, on every action performed on window or anyother components.

Button: Buttons are used to execute some operation on the widow. On pushing the button down, it execute some set of code. Let's see an example of how to generate button.

Script

```
use Tkx;

#Creating Window

$mw=Tkx::widget->new(".");

$mw->g_wm_title("Hello");

$mw->g_wm_minsize(300,300);

$mw->g_wm_resizable(1,1);
```

```
#Creating Button
$b=$mw->new_button(
        -text => "Hello, world",
        -command => \&destroy);
$b->g_pack();

$b1=$mw->new_button(
        -text => "Tip",
        -command => sub {

      Tkx::tk___messageBox(-parent => $mw,-icon
=> "info",-title => "Tip of the Day", -message
=> "Please be nice!");
                                           });
$b1->g_pack(-padx=>30,-pady=>50,-side=>"left");
Tkx::MainLoop();

sub destroy
{
      $b->m_configure(-text => "Goodbye, cruel
world");
      Tkx::after(1000, sub { $mw->g_destroy });
}
```

Output

```
G:\Programs\Perl\GUI>perl pg2.pl
```

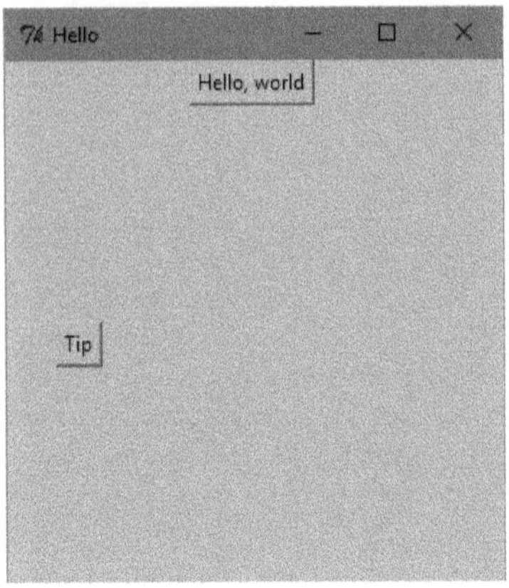

There is another new statement in the script which is **`Tkx::tk___messageBox(-parent => $mw,-icon => "info",-title => "Tip of the Day", -message => "Please be nice!");`** which creates a message dialog box with message "Please be nice".

The **g_pack()** method only attaches the respective button to the respective window. The **`g_destroy()`** method as name suggests destroys the respective window. The **`m_configure()`** method is used to make some changes on button such as text. The **`after()`** method perform a certain action after specified milliseconds (here 1000 milliseconds or 10 seconds).

Label: Labels are used to display message on the window. The labels are quite useful to guide the user while used along with text box. Let's now see how to create a label, it's similar to that of button, but the name is label.

Script

```
use Tkx;

#Creating Window

$mw=Tkx::widget->new(".");

$mw->g_wm_title("Hello");

$mw->g_wm_minsize(300,100);

$mw->g_wm_resizable(1,1);

#Creating Label

$label=$mw->new_label(-text=>"Hello You",-
font=>"Consolas 30 bold italic");

$label->g_pack();

Tkx::MainLoop();
```

Output

```
G:\Programs\Perl\GUI>perl pg3.pl
```

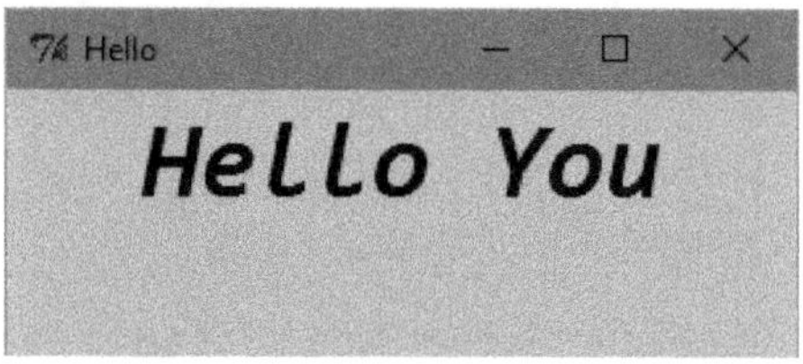

The label can also be configured using a method called **`$label->configure(-text=>TEXT);`** which we will see in forth coming examples.

The rule for font alter in the label is "FONTNAME SIZE STYLE"

Frames: Frame is a primary widget or a container to hold other components. The Frames are created to separate the information on screen mixing from one another.

Script

```
use Tkx;

#Creating Window

$mw=Tkx::widget->new(".");

$mw->g_wm_title("Hello");

$mw->g_wm_minsize(300,100);

$mw->g_wm_resizable(1,1);

#Creating Frame 1

$frame1=$mw->new_frame();

$frame1->g_pack();

#Creating Frame 2

$frame2=$mw->new_frame(-background=>"#FFFFFF");

$frame2->g_pack();

#Creating Label on Frame1

$label=$frame1->new_label(-text=>"Hello You",-
font=>"Consolas 30 bold italic",-
relief=>"groove");

$label->g_pack();

#Creating Button on Main Window

$b1=$frame2->new_button(-text => "Exit",-
command => sub {$mw->g_destroy();});
```

```
$b1->g_pack(-padx=>100,-pady=>30,-
side=>"right");

Tkx::MainLoop();
```

Output

```
G:\Programs\Perl\GUI>perl pg4.pl
```

Text Area (box): Text area are used to get information from the user, like reading from console or terminal. To ensure correct information are entered in text area make sure text box are accompanied by labels.

Script

```
use Tkx;

#Creating Window

$mw=Tkx::widget->new(".");

$mw->g_wm_title("Hello");

$mw->g_wm_minsize(300,150);

$mw->g_wm_resizable(1,1);

#Creating Frame

$frame1=$mw->new_frame();
```

```
$frame1->g_pack();

#Creating Label on Frame

$label=$frame1->new_label(-text=>"Hello You",-
font=>"Consolas 30 bold italic",-
relief=>"groove");

$label->g_pack();

#Creating Button on Frame

$b1=$frame1->new_button(-text => "Push me",-
command =>\&push_button);

$b1->g_pack();

#Creating Button on Frame

$b2=$frame1->new_button(-text => "Exit",-
command =>sub {$mw->g_destroy();});

$b2->g_pack();

#Text Area

$txt = $mw->new_tk__text(-width=>15,-
height=>1);

$txt->g_pack();

Tkx::MainLoop();


sub push_button

{

      my $name = $txt->get("1.0","end");

      $txt->delete("1.0","2.0");
```

```
        $txt->insert("1.5 linestart","Hello,
$name");
}
```

Output

```
G:\Programs\Perl\GUI>perl pg5.pl
```

Like configuring the labels and button, the text box can be configured using methods such as, **get(LINENUMBER, WHERE)** or **delete(LINENUM_START, LINENUM_END)** or **insert(LINENUM, TEXT)** to modify data inside the text box. For inserting or getting data from start .5 is added to line number.

Radio Button: Radio Button are quite useful when only one option has to be chosen when 'n' options are provided. Changing the option will lose the previous selected state. The radio button are grouped by using variable. Let's see an example:

Script

```
use Tkx;

#Creating Window
```

```
$mw=Tkx::widget->new(".");

$mw->g_wm_title("Hello");

$mw->g_wm_minsize(300,150);

$mw->g_wm_resizable(1,1);

#Creating Frame

$frame1=$mw->new_frame();

$frame1->g_pack();

#Creating Radio Button

$gender="Male";

$radio_m=$frame1->new_radiobutton(-
text=>"Male",-value=>"Male",-
variable=>\$gender);

$radio_m->g_pack();

$radio_f=$frame1->new_radiobutton(-
text=>"Female",-value=>"Female",-
variable=>\$gender);

$radio_f->g_pack();

#Creating Button

$b1=$frame1->new_button(-text  =>  "Push  me",-
command =>\&push_button);

$b1->g_pack();

#Creating Label

$label=$mw->new_label(-text=>"$gender",-
font=>"Consolas    30    bold    italic",-
relief=>"groove");
```

```
$label->g_pack();
Tkx::MainLoop();


sub push_button
{
	$label->configure(-text=>"$gender");
}
```

Output

```
G:\Programs\Perl\GUI>perl pg6.pl
```

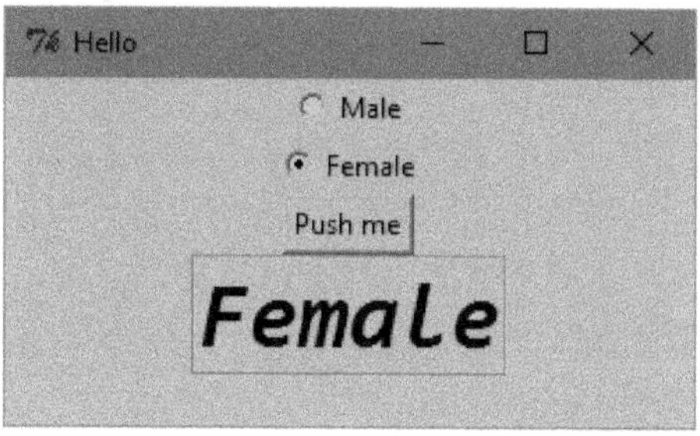

Checkbox: Checkbox are useful when multiple options has to be chosen. The state changes on checking the box on. The checkbox are bound by separate variable.

Script

```
use Tkx;
#Creating Window
$mw=Tkx::widget->new(".");
$mw->g_wm_title("Hello");
```

```
$mw->g_wm_minsize(300,150);

$mw->g_wm_resizable(1,1);

#Creating Checkbox

$bike=1;

$car=1;

$chk=$mw->new_ttk__checkbutton(-text=>"Bike",-
variable=>\$bike);

$chk->g_pack();

$chk1=$mw->new_ttk__checkbutton(-text=>"Car",-
variable=>\$car);

$chk1->g_pack();

Tkx::MainLoop();
```

Output

```
G:\Programs\Perl\GUI>perl pg7.pl
```

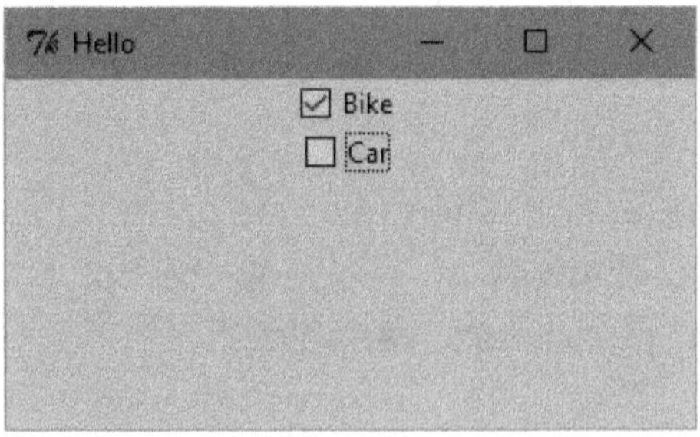

If the variable has value '1' then the check box is shown with a tick mark. In the above picture I manually unchecked for Car.

Using the values in the variable we can obtain information for each context.

<u>Combo box:</u> The combo box are used when the list of option available is more, in such cases radio buttons require more lines of code. Such cases combo boxes plays a vital role. Let's see an example:

<u>Script</u>

```
use Tkx;

#Creating Window

$mw=Tkx::widget->new(".");

$mw->g_wm_title("Hello");

$mw->g_wm_minsize(300,150);

$mw->g_wm_resizable(1,1);

#Creating Combo box

$day="Monday";

$cb=$mw->new_ttk__combobox(-textvariable=>
\$day,);

$cb->g_pack();

$cb->configure(-values=>"Monday Tuesday
Wednesday Thursday Friday Saturday Sunday");

Tkx::MainLoop();
```

<u>Output</u>

```
G:\Programs\Perl\GUI>perl pg8.pl
```

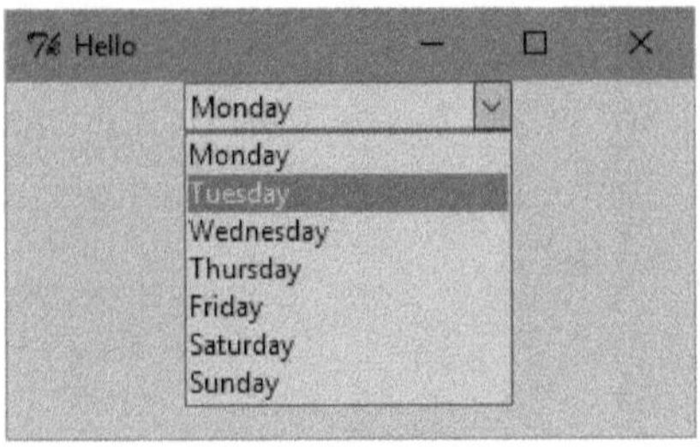

The variable contains the changed value, which can be accessed for later use.

Menu: Menu is one such widget that can contain list of commands that can be grouped under a similar name. Menus helps to conserve space availability for screen. Menu are contained on the top layer of the window. Let's see how to create menu:

Script

```
use Tkx;

#Creating Window

$mw=Tkx::widget->new(".");

$mw->g_wm_title("Hello");

$mw->g_wm_minsize(100,100);

$mw->g_wm_resizable(1,1);

#Creating Menu

Tkx::option_add("*tearOff", 0);

$menu=$mw->new_menu();
```

```
$mw->configure(-menu=>$menu);

$file=$menu->new_menu();

$menu->add_cascade(-menu=>$file,-
label=>"File",-underline=>0);

$file->add_command(-label=>"Message",-
underline=>1,-command=>sub {


      Tkx::tk___messageBox(-parent => $mw,-icon
=> "info",-title => "Tip of the Day", -message
=> "Please be nice!"); });

$file->add_separator();

$file->add_command(-label=>"Exit",-
underline=>0,-command=>sub{$mw->g_destroy();});

Tkx::MainLoop();
```

Output

```
G:\Programs\Perl\GUI>perl pg9.pl
```

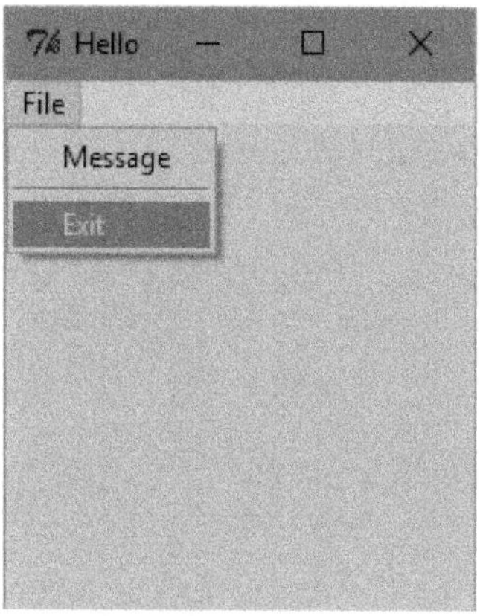

The **add_separator()** function creates a line between two commands.

Let’s see a Temperature convertor application along with script:

Script

```
use Tkx;

#Creating Window

$mw=Tkx::widget->new(".");

$mw->g_wm_title("Temperature Convertor");

$mw->g_wm_minsize(300,80);

$mw->g_wm_resizable(0,0);

#Creating Label

$label=$mw->new_label(-text=>"Enter temperature
in C  ",-font=>"Calibri 11 bold");

$label->g_grid(-row=>1,-column=>1);

#Text Area

$txt = $mw->new_tk__text(-width=>20,-
height=>1);

$txt->g_grid(-row=>1,-column=>2);

#Creating Button

$b=$mw->new_button(-text => "Convert", -command
=> \&convert);

$b->g_grid(-row=>2,-column=>2);

#Creating Label

$f=0;
```

```
$label1=$mw->new_label(-text=>"",-
font=>"Calibri 11 bold");

$label1->g_grid(-row=>2,-column=>1);

Tkx::MainLoop();


sub convert

{

      my $val = $txt->get("1.0","end");

      if($val=~/^-?\d*\.?\d*$/)

      {

            $f=($val*9)/5 + 32;

            $label1->configure(-text=>"In
Farenheit is $f F");

      }

      else

      {

            Tkx::tk___messageBox(-parent =>
$mw,-icon => "info",-title => "Please Enter the
correct value", -message => "Entered is not a
valid number!!");

      }

}
```

Output

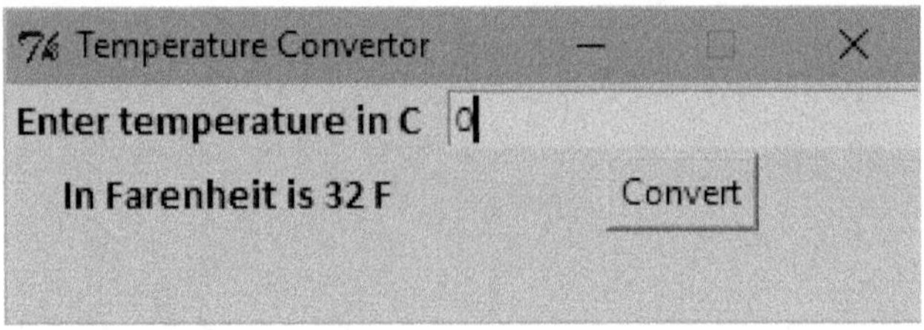
Temperature Convertor
Enter temperature in C
0
In Farenheit is 32 F
Convert

INDEX

www.ingramcontent.com/pod-product-compliance
Lightning Source LLC
LaVergne TN
LVHW022302060326
832902LV00020B/3230
* 9 7 8 1 5 3 0 9 5 9 6 3 1 *